why animals sleep
so close to the road
(and other lies
I tell my children)

why animals

sleep so close to

the road

SUSAN KONIG

(and other lies
I tell my children)

Thomas Dunne Books

St. Martin's Press   New York

THOMAS DUNNE BOOKS
An imprint of St. Martin's Press

www.stmartins.com

ISBN 0-312-33236-X
EAN 978-0312-33236-5

First Edition: May 2005

10   9   8   7   6   5   4   3   2   1

For my husband and our children.

For my mother,
who taught me how to be a mom.

And for my father,
who taught me how to lie about dead pets.

contents

acknowledgments

I would like to thank the following people who helped make this book possible:

My agent, Jack Scovil.

My publisher, Tom Dunne, and my editor, Anne Merrow.

John Podhoretz, who gave me a column and told me to write whatever I wanted.

Nina Hyde, who taught me how to write for a newspaper.

The city moms—Karen, Lucia, and Debbi.

The suburban moms—Julia, Sue Ellen, and Pennie.

The Boltin/VanHagen writers' colony and babysitting service.

Ta and Carlo, everybody's favorite aunt and uncle.

All my friends and family who encouraged me.

prologue

Bambi's mother was just running an errand

I lie to my kids. Not just sometimes—all the time. I'm a big stinky liar. Sure, sure, it's important to tell your kids the truth. Except when it's better to just flat out lie.

This approach automatically applies to all Disney films. Take *The Lion King*, for instance. Simba's father was not, as it appeared, crushed to death in front of his cub. He's just resting at the bottom of the gorge until the stampede is over and will probably meet up with his son in a sequel. Tarzan's parents weren't eaten alive by a cheetah while he slept in his crib. They were probably just knocked unconscious and will meet up with their son in a sequel. The meteorite that crashes to Earth in *Dinosaur* merely set fire to an island and didn't de-

stroy the entire population of the planet except for one dinosaur and four monkeys. All the other animals swam away
and will probably meet up in a sequel. Disney has a formula
for children; I have a formula for Disney.

But there are other, real-life situations that call for fudging
the facts. For example, if we're driving around the country-
side (read "suburbs") and see the occasional animal lying mo-
tionless at the edge of the highway, I'll yell out, "Hey, is that
the moon?" so everyone will look up (even my husband falls
for this one) and the children won't see the poor creature. It's
a diversionary tactic. Sometimes one of the kids, bless them,
will actually find the moon and make an honest woman of
me.

But once, I was distracted, paying attention to my driving or
looking at road signs, and from her booster car-seat vantage
point, my then four-year-old daughter piped up, "Momma,
why do animals sleep so close to the road?"

Now what was I to do? Blurt out, "That raccoon's not
sleeping. It's dead. It's obviously been struck by a vehicle going in excess of 60 miles per hour. Probably an SUV." I don't
think so. Instead I said something like, "Gee, that's a good
question. We'll have to look into that. You'd think they'd be
scared, but maybe they're so used to the sound of cars that
they can fall asleep anywhere."

And who got hurt in this scenario (besides the raccoon)?
No one.

I also lie about where Christmas trees go after they are put
out by the curb. Santa's special garbage trucks pick them up

and bring them back up to the North Pole, where they're re-animated for the next year.

I lie about meat. I told the kids that the chicken and beef we eat comes from cows and chickens that died of old age.

These are just some of the useful skills I've learned while walking the parenthood beat. But I wasn't always this quick. I had to learn about roadkill and the suburbs. Having grown up in New York City, I already had the Santa tree thing worked out. You do the best you can. Being a mom's an ongoing (and dishonest) process.

Kids have their whole lives to know about bad stuff, sad stuff, scary stuff, even mildly upsetting stuff. They don't want to know that the tree they lovingly decorated and found gifts underneath on Christmas morning is going to a dump. They don't even want to know that it's preventing erosion at some beach. Recycling, though it's drummed into their heads in every single cartoon, is not that important to them.

And they probably don't want to know that, back in the old country, their great grandmother used to swing chickens over her head to break their necks. I don't even want to know that.

They have questions, and we need to be ready with answers. What does the Tooth Fairy do with all those teeth? (Builds Tooth Fairy castles.) Where does the Sandman get his sand? (Jones Beach.) Where do babies come from? (Chinatown or Macy's—depends on the baby.)

Right now, their dad and I and the other grown-ups who love them can act as buffers until we just can't buffer anymore. We're the ones who are supposed to lie awake at night worrying about the national debt and deforestation and wildlife mortality rates. They are supposed to have sweet dreams and visits from the Sandman and no bites from bed-bugs.

That's the job and I aim to do it.

why animals sleep

so close to the road

(and other lies

I tell my children)

I

the family that stays together
(in a really small apartment)
prays for more space

Why were my kids so uninformed about roadkill? They'd spent their entire young lives living in the big city. But all that was about to change.

It all began rather innocently as my husband and I weighed the pros and cons of apartment life. We were in a prewar doorman building on the Upper East Side of Manhattan—a good location as those things go. For instance, shopping was easy enough, if you call toting bags of groceries while wrangling two kids under five across busy intersections full of insane bus drivers and pushy pedestrians who want to play chicken with the harried mother "easy." But we were just a block away from my mother, who lived in the same apartment she always had, the one my sister and I had grown up in.

Our two-bedroom apartment was ridiculously small—but is ridiculously small necessarily bad?

Our living room was twelve feet by nineteen and a half feet on a good day, and it was crowded. My "office" was in the living room. The dining room was in the living room. The family room was in the living room. The living room was in the living room. So were the TV, the high chair, the playpen, and the kitchen stool.

Unless we were out of our apartment or sleeping in our teeny, tiny bedrooms (conveniently located just off the living room), there were four of us in the living room: my husband, our two kids, and me. And now there was more of me since I was pregnant with our third child. Oh, and we had a cat. There was an excessive amount of living in that living room.

There were pluses. Living in such a tiny space meant I could avoid actually waking up when our preschooler climbed out of bed early in the morning and asked if she could watch *Sesame Street*. I'd sleepwalk to the kitchen just a few feet away and give her a cup of dry cereal. She knew how to work the remote so I'd go back to bed, dozing and needing only to open my eyes to see her sitting on the couch, munching Cheerios, and singing, *"Uno, dos, tres, cuatro, cinco, seis . . ."*

I could cook in the kitchen and be fully aware of where everyone was in the apartment. A previous tenant, recognizing the limits of space in apartment 10A, had installed a lot of mirrors on various walls, trying to create the illusion that the apartment was actually bigger than it was. The far wall in the living room was mirrored floor to ceiling, and even the backsplash to the kitchen sink was a mirror. This enabled me to truly convince my children that I had eyes in the back of my head. "Stop jabbing your brother with that salad fork," I'd say, standing at the kitchen sink, and their little mouths would drop open.

I could leap from any location in the apartment and, in a single step, keep our toddler son from plunging off the "dining room" table (in the living room). The Flying Wallendas would have been proud of both of us.

There was also a downside that had a lot to do with size versus price—we were paying a fortune in rent for what my husband called "this dump" where the kids were "stacked up like cordwood." Neighbors were never shy about saying, upon first seeing our apartment, "Why, this must be the smallest unit in the building. It doesn't even have a maid's room." That was the beauty part because we didn't have a maid.

Two adults in the kitchen simultaneously were enough to set off a small-scale marital crisis. Add a kid or two and you had a full-blown claustrophobia-induced nervous breakdown. Remember Cary Grant and Myrna Loy going nuts in their cramped Manhattan apartment in *Mr. Blandings Builds His Dream House?* They had nothing on us. Life in the Konig household was about as spacious and comfortable as a sarcophagus for a minor member of Egyptian royalty in a poor century when they were cutting corners in the sarcophagus industry.

There were other negatives, too, but I don't want to brag. Unfortunately, our already astronomical rent crept up to the equivalent of the gross national product of a small European nation per month, and our family size was about to creep up to include a new baby. I was sure we were going to have to move.

My husband kept talking about looking at houses outside the city, but I had my heart set on staying put and raising my kids the way I was raised. Having always lived in the city and always in apartments, I never envisioned myself doing otherwise. He was skeptical about being able to afford a large Manhattan apartment. "You'll see," I told him. "I'll find us something."

Unfortunately, in my unrealistic mind's eye, I'd always imagined that we'd eventually end up in a sitcom apartment—one of those impossibly large lofts or a rambling prewar apartment with fourteen rooms. Everyone on TV always has a huge, spacious apartment, capable of housing a large family, three cameras, and a studio audience. I always assumed someday I would, too.

2

# of mice and me

Just as I was thinking that maybe we could tough it out in our tiny, overpriced apartment for a while, even after the new baby arrived, it became more crowded. Once again our home was filled with the pitter-patter of little feet—little mice feet.

Or mouse. I liked to think that it was always the same one and that he was very busy, scampering here and there, enjoying the warmth of the radiator in our living room, curiously exploring the kitchen, stopping only to gaze at us quizzically with his little black eyes, twitch his pink ears, stick out his mousy tongue.

We'd never had this problem before. Well, once. A couple of years earlier. Right after our son was born, a friend was in from California and wanted to stop by and see how we were enjoying our bon vivant existence on the fashionable Upper East Side. As we sat chatting in the living room, our guest said, "Looks like Scout has a friend."

Scout, our good fine cat, was under a cabinet in the living room playing with a mouse. But Scoutie wasn't getting any younger, and she just didn't have the killer instincts anymore. She would hunt and play and . . . release. The mouse stared in disbelief at my old cat, surprised to be free, shrugged his little mouse shoulders, and zipped off. Scout just sighed and took another nap.

We looked at that as a freak occurrence. The super came up and plugged some holes under our heaters with steel wool, and that was that.

But this time, workmen on scaffolding were jackhammering outside our windows. They were replacing all the window ledges in the building. They liked to start right outside our bedroom window every morning. For many days in a row. With jackhammers. I did mention they had jackhammers, didn't I?

It seems all this nerve-jangling activity upset the delicate balance of mouse life that existed in the hidden world behind our apartment walls. In a jackhammer-induced frenzy, they ripped through the steel wool and invaded our apartment. And I'm not talking middle-of-the-night sneaking around. These guys were brazen! They came out in the daytime and ran through the living room with not a care in the world, as though they were chipping in on the rent. They'd make a break for the kitchen and do that running-in-place Warner Bros. cartoon thing where they slide on the floor because it's a sharp turn and then skitter behind the refrigerator.

I looked for sympathy in all the wrong places. There was my sister, the nature lover, who, since we were kids, has caught houseflies under a glass and freed them with a flourish and a hearty farewell at the window. I called her one night because I was trapped in a human-to-mouse standoff and my husband was out and the kids were asleep. The mouse kept trying to come out from underneath the radiator, and I kept stamping my foot and saying, "No! You get back there, you . . . you mouse!" or stronger words to that effect.

My sister told me that the one time she had found a mouse in her house, it had fallen asleep on her folded jeans. She gently picked it up—"I think he was feeling unwell"—and slowly carried the mouse on its bed of denim to a nearby park, where she reintroduced him to the natural world.

I just wanted to know what would be more effective, whacking the annoying pest with a broom or a mop? The mouse, that is, not my sister.

My husband came home and, in his adorably impulsive way, said, "That's it. Where are those glue traps?" The super had left some when he plugged our holes. I told my husband he would have to deal with the consequences and hoped the mouse would step around a gluey fate.

About 11:00 p.m. we were sitting around watching the news and we heard struggling. Right behind us. Of course, in this apartment, everything was right behind us.

I can't really go into what happened next; it's too upsetting. Suffice it to say that it involved crying, screaming, cursing, squeaking, an umbrella, a bucket, a plastic bag, a wire hanger, and an open window. Finally my husband gave up, and I disposed of the annoying pest. The mouse, that is, not my husband.

3

mouse redux

Our period of mourning and recovery was cut short by the appearance of an identical mouse traveling the same path several mornings later, like the ghost of some murdered relative haunting the killers in an Émile Zola novel.

The exterminator, endearingly referred to by my children as Bug Man, arrived to say that our holes were too numerous to plug. He tossed some poison packets behind our cabinets where the mice had been living it up and told me that I probably wouldn't hear from them after about a week. They'd munch this apple-flavored stuff and go gently into that good night.

Then things got ugly. As we continued to argue and debate the situation with our landlord, our super, our super's assistant, the building exterminator, and anyone else who'd listen, I went through the five stages of coping with rodentia: fear, anger, denial, a lot of screaming, and, finally, acceptance. What was the big deal? So we saw the occasional mouse in our apartment. These things happen. But our little critter started bringing his friends in on the deal and finally, one night, they were everywhere. I felt like Ray Milland with the DTs in *The Lost Weekend*, when he kept seeing mice all over the place.

I also felt like Ray Milland in *The Man with the X-ray Eyes*, when he had X-ray vision and it drove him crazy because he kept seeing stuff he didn't want to see, just like how I kept seeing mice all over the place. I also felt like Ray Milland in *The Man with Two Heads*, when for some reason he had two heads and one of them was Rosie Greer's. (Okay, that has nothing to do with mice, but he was upset that he had two heads and I was upset that my apartment was filled with mice.)

Late that night my husband was busy cursing our anti-mouse electronic device that had cost seventy dollar and was supposed to make an undetectable-to-human-ears noise that mice can't stand. Well, they came out from under the heater and did a little dance in front of our space-age weaponry just to show that they had no respect for our puny human technology.

I told my beleaguered spouse to come into the bedroom and let the mice have their little fun scampering around the kitchen. I figured that since our room was the only one with a light on they'd stay out there in the dark. Within minutes, however, I looked down and saw this little son of a gun waltzing through our bedroom without a care in the world. I knew my husband wasn't going to handle this well. Softly, I got his attention. "Honey . . ."

With an edge in his voice that can only be the product of an evening of mouse hunting, he said, "What?" But he was really saying, "In the name of all that's holy, please don't tell me what I think you're going to tell me."

The little pest froze (the mouse, not my husband). I grabbed a literary magazine, aimed carefully, and fired away. I was just trying to scare it, not kill it. To kill I'd need at least the March *Vogue,* the spring fashion issue, or maybe a bridal magazine. Anyway, I missed.

Needless to say we got no sleep, though we did make valuable use of our nonsleeping time by "catching" and "disposing of" two mice before dawn. It wasn't pretty. But details would only make PETA come after us.

I asked my husband if he wouldn't concede that one of the great things about living in the city, which we'd discovered that night, is that you can walk across the street and buy mouse traps at 1:00 a.m. He told me that one of the great things about moving to the suburbs is that we wouldn't have a mouse problem in the first place. And we'd be in a nice big house instead of a small, cramped apartment that costs an arm and a leg. I decided to shut up.

4

throwing up walls

We were renters. My husband wanted to buy a house in the suburbs. I wanted to stay in an apartment in the city. So I decided, as a compromise, we would buy an apartment in the city.

I began the search for a three-bedroom apartment and quickly found that our budget only allowed for a two-bedroom "plus," as in "plus" a little something extra. For instance, a two-bedroom plus a dining room where we could "throw up a wall" (as the Realtors put it) and make it a third bedroom. They glossed over the fact that someone would then be sleeping in the dining room except for that wall and we'd have to walk through a bedroom to get from the kitchen to the living room.

Or perhaps we'd find a two-bedroom plus a maid's room but that would mean that one of the kids would be relegated to sleeping in back of the kitchen. That's kind of scary for a small child. But it would be equally scary for my husband and me. We were certainly not going to get stuck in that cramped excuse for a room.

Or we'd look at a big two-bedroom and I'd convince myself we could divide the larger bedroom into two. You know, throw up a wall. I badgered my husband until he was sold on the idea. But when he came to look at the apartment he said, "And which child won't have a window?" I cheerfully suggested that we could divide the room down the center of the window so each child could have a sliver of light. He nodded "So which one doesn't get a door?"

Most of the properties we looked at were either on deserted scary blocks far from grocery stores or on busy avenues with bus stops out front and virtually no security. Most were on the first floor. One was in a buzzer building, but it was the only apartment in the building where the door was before the buzzer, which meant people could directly approach without having to be buzzed in. Even the super refused to live in that apartment.

And all of the substandard apartments with windowless, doorless, or nonexistent third bedrooms were about a couple hundred thousand dollars more than we two artistic types could afford anyway. They were also co-ops, that strange New York City invention that requires owners to pay a high monthly maintenance on top of the huge mortgage that we couldn't afford in the first place.

After a few weeks of apartment shopping, I used the razor-sharp skills I'd learned as a journalist for considering and evaluating a particular situation, to come to this unique conclusion: three-bedroom apartments in Manhattan are really, really expensive.

5

---

do you know
where your children are?

As if to punctuate our debate over the city versus the suburbs, I misplaced my son in Central Park. Central Park in New York City. My son who was just twenty-three months old.

We were at the sprinkler in the playground. Three moms, three four-year-olds, and my little guy. The older kids filled their buckets and began their favorite game of chasing and splashing each other while all three moms watched my son because he's so young. We took pictures, mostly of him. We started talking about something. I'm sure I was doing most of the talking. And then he was gone.

"Where is he?"

Nobody answered me.

"Where is he?"

I scanned the playground. I asked my daughter, "Where is he?"

She knew something was wrong. She began to cry, "My mommy lost my brother!" Why weren't the other moms answering me? They were looking too, as hard as they could. From where we stood we could see the whole playground, so we froze, our eyes frantically searching. I was calling his name. Finally one mom said, "It's a gated park, he's not gone." But where was he? "He's wearing a diaper, no shirt," I heard the other mom tell somebody.

I couldn't see him. There were so many kids, I couldn't focus. Finally, after about ninety seconds, I spotted him at the top of the play fort, ready to go down the curly slide. He's not allowed to climb that high. I leapt up to him in what felt like one motion. I grabbed him, carried him down, toweled him off, and put on a shirt and a dry diaper. I apologized to my daughter for scaring her. "We're going," I said. My back started spasming—that'd never happened before. I was too nauseous to cry.

I kept it together until my husband called home that afternoon. My daughter picked up. "Hi, Daddy, Mommy lost my little brother in the park today, but she found him. 'Bye." She handed me the phone.

"Did you lose one of our children today?" my husband asked, sounding hopeful that I would contradict our daughter.

My voice was shaky, "I was right there. He was right in front of me. I don't know how it happened. . . ." Then I cried.

I'd spent every waking hour trying to protect the kids, and I'd failed miserably. I'd even made it a point to stop and talk to police on the street and tell the kids that an officer would always help them. We had gone to the firehouse to say hello to the firefighters. I had reminded the children of the nice salesladies and store clerks around the neighborhood who knew them and could help them if they were lost or somebody was bothering them. I had told my daughter to hold her brother's hand, keep an eye on him, show him how we cross the street. Always hold hands. "No," he said.

I had tried to introduce the idea of an emergency situation. How my daughter could dial 911 if anything ever happened to me or if she was all alone or I got sick or she was in trouble. "But that's never going to happen," I had told her. "I'll take care of you. But just in case."

She was cooler than I was because she had told me they have fire drills at nursery school, and she knew to get out and never go back in even for the cat because animals usually know what to do and probably could get out or a firefighter could go in and save the cat. Then she had dropped to her knees and said, "This is how you go if there's smoke. You crawl out. And if you get on fire you do this." And she sang, "Stop, drop, and roll." She got that one from TV.

She could recite our phone number perfectly, but only if she repeated our machine's entire greeting, "You have reached——Please leave a message after the beep." She knew her name and address and her grandmother's name and address two blocks away.

After the playground incident, those other moms and I started a mom's night out once a month so we could talk without rushing and being interrupted. So I wouldn't get *so* caught up in my own fascinating discourse that I'd lose track of my kids. So we could recharge our batteries enough to get back to the joyful but unrelenting responsibilities of being moms.

Maybe life would be simpler, safer in the suburbs. . . .

6

confessions of a (former) party girl

But I wasn't quite ready to throw in the towel on my largely imagined cosmopolitan existence.

"Can we go canoodling at Moomba?" I asked my husband one night.

"No."

"You don't even know what it is."

"Canoodling or Moomba?"

"Moomba."

"What is it?"

"It's an 'in' place where people canoodle."

"What's a canoodle?"

"I'm not quite sure."

"No."

"But I want to go canoodling at Moomba."

"Go with Lulu."

Of course! My former partner in crime from the good old days when I actually had a reason to put on black clothes and leave my apartment at 11:00 p.m., which is a half hour later than my current bedtime.

When single girl Lulu came over to play with the kids, I asked her, "Want to go canoodling at Moomba?"

"We can't canoodle. That's kissing, right?"

"I'm not sure. But we can see and be seen and find out who's canoodling. Maybe you'll meet someone to canoodle with, and I can go home early."

"Okay. How do we get in?"

"I don't know. We walk in."

"I don't think so. I'm not in the mood to be rejected at the velvet rope."

"Do they still do that?"

"Oh, you've been home a long time."

"But we used to get in. We'd just go in."

"We were young, thin, hip . . ."

"Well, we're still . . ."

She put up her hand.

"Why are you putting your hand in my face?" I asked.

"Talk to the hand."

"Talk to the hand?"

"Talk to the hand."

"What does that mean, 'Talk to the hand?' "

"You've never heard 'Talk to the hand?' "

"Do 4-year-olds say it?"

Over the next couple of weeks we read the columns to keep tabs on who was canoodling with whom at Moomba and elsewhere. Not a person over thirty in the lot. And no average schmoes either.

I began to reconsider the need to make the scene. "I know what you mean," Lulu agreed, when she called from her office one afternoon. "This whole canoodling thing seems like it takes more effort than I thought."

"Yeah, and I don't even own a cell phone! Want to come over to my place and eat ice cream and watch a movie instead?"

"I'll come up after work on Friday."

We rented *Breakfast at Tiffany's* and, once the kids were asleep and my husband had retreated to the bedroom to listen to the Mets game on the radio and avoid girl talk, we sat on the couch eating Ben & Jerry's and popcorn.

"So where is Moomba anyway?"

"I think it's downtown."

"Quel cab fare! Do they serve food?"

"I don't know. Pass the popcorn."

"Wouldn't you love to look like that in the morning?" sighed Lulu over a breathtaking Audrey Hepburn as Holly Golightly, complete with bejeweled earplugs and sequined sleep mask.

"She's a movie star," I said. "They made her look that way. Besides, all twenty-something party girls look that good. We looked that good when we were party girls."

We weren't the couture-wearing, limo-hopping, cell phone kind of party girls, but we used to smoke and be thin and go out every night. Granted, we hung out at a dive bar downtown and drank Bud and danced to a band called the Worms. But it was always a party, and we *were* girls. We often came home at sunrise. That was fun.

"But Holly Golightly was a gamine," Lulu protests. "We're not gamines."

"Speak for yourself. I'm a gamine. A 160-pound, big-boned, Irish, married mother-of-two-and-a-half gamine."

"What happened to us?" asked Lulu, between spoonfuls of ice cream straight from the container.

"Well, all that smoking gave me bronchitis. But really, we stepped aside."

"We did?"

"Sure. All party girls have to give it up sometime to make room for the new batch. Maybe soon some real party girls will step up to the plate and make it fun again. But it's no longer our problem—our canoodling days are over."

"Amen. Now shut up and pass the Cherry Garcia. She's singing 'Moon River.' "

7

mom's hobby

They say Harriet Beecher Stowe wrote *Uncle Tom's Cabin* with a bunch of kids running around the kitchen table. Maybe it's a myth, but at least her husband wasn't sitting five feet away watching reruns of *I Love Lucy*.

I was in the bedroom trying to write longhand in a notebook because my husband was a few feet away in the living room (also my office), which was where my computer was. He was watching a *Lucy* episode he'd seen 132 times. People, and that includes husbands, just don't take you seriously if you work at home, squeezing in work during off hours. When he came home, my husband couldn't resist the old, "Another day of bonbons and soap operas, eh?" It was a joke, but it wore a little thin. My friends said, "Oh, I'd love to stay home all day." Yes, they knew I was raising kids and working on the side, but the implication of the comment was that I was lazy. I could work in my pajamas, but it was still work. They didn't understand that.

"You can do it later," said my husband, who didn't really mean to undermine my work but wanted me to join him on the couch that evening. I wanted to relax and watch reruns, too, but, unfortunately, my job was not stuffing envelopes. Freelance writing took a little concentration that I didn't have anyway after taking care of the kids all day. It was hard to summon up that kind of energy if (A) I sat on a soft bed full of fluffy pillows instead of at my desk in a wooden chair, (B) I was tense and exasperated because no one was supporting my creative process, and (C) it was the one with Bill Holden where Lucy sets fire to her nose.

I used to have a normal working schedule, and I remember it fondly. When I worked in an office, life was very relaxing. I'd roll in with coffee and a muffin, maybe look at the newspaper, check in with coworkers to see how everyone was doing, do a little typing in peace and solitude, make a few phone calls, make lunch plans, open the mail, go freshen up in the ladies' room, go out for a relaxing lunch, window shop, do a little more work, order out for an afternoon cappuccino fix, make after-work plans, and watch the clock until five. I'd get paid to take personal days; sick days; doctor, dentist, manicurist, and reflexologist appointments. It was good. Sure, occasionally I'd get fired, but that would just give me more time to have lunch, window shop, and sip cappuccino.

Later, as a freelancer, it wasn't as cushy—no one was paying me when I wasn't working—but it was sane. I slept late. I could roll out of bed, fire up the old computer, line up my business calls, do a phone interview. Or I could throw on jeans and a T-shirt, mosey out for coffee and a muffin, brush my cat, watch a soap opera, drink Tab, and smoke cigarettes. But I could always sit down and work for five, six, or seven hours uninterrupted, even if it meant staying up half the night.

Those days were over. Back in *I Love Lucy* land, it was Saturday and my husband wanted to help out. "Okay," he said, "I'm taking the kids to the park so you can work. Get them dressed and we'll be out of your hair in no time. I'm taking a shower."

Here's the problem with this setup: I didn't want to get the kids ready. I didn't want my husband to "help out." I wanted him to take over—completely. I'd had it. But I took what I could get and filled them full of Cheerios, washed the sticky parts, and cajoled and wrestled them into clothes. And I filled bottles and sippy cups because my husband had that father's disease of not being able to screw on the tops right and juice would leak all over the kids, who'd then have to be changed, and we know who is in charge of dressing them.

So they were going and I was zipping jackets and giving instructions and no one was listening to me. As they left, my husband said, "Now you just work. And if you get a chance, can you run the vacuum around?"

I took a moment to remind myself that homicide is illegal. Then I ignored that last part because I had to work and I had maybe an hour to myself and no time to shower or make a call. If I wanted to get anything done, I had to put my marital issues aside. So I popped in some early '80s music (Stevie Winwood) and pretended I was still single. That made it a little better and I got to work.

I got a nice four-hour-old cup of coffee from the pot and sat down to write. I rarely brought anything to drink over to my desk because there was no place to put down a cup. And, usually, the kids were marauding and I was afraid they'd spill something on my keyboard.

But this day it was just me and I needed a jump start and I put the coffee cup down on the mouse pad and I pushed the mouse out of the way because, after all, I was just going to type. Before I let go of the cup handle, I chuckled to myself about how I could never do this in front of the kids because I was always telling them "Don't do that" and "It's going to spill." But I was doing it because I was an adult, and I knew how to get through the day without knocking stuff over. So I let go. I put my hands on the keyboard for exactly one second, then, out of sheer force or stupid habit, I moved my right hand to where the bleeding mouse should have been because I wanted to move the bloody cursor, and I knocked the coffee full force off the desk, soaking my surge protector and staining my white carpeting (which was a joint stupid decision I'd made with my husband—look for my new book *Only a Complete Moron Would Buy White Carpeting with Two Kids and Other Seemingly Obvious Observations*, in stores soon).

I shut everything down really quickly so that I wouldn't get electrocuted, cursing like an overtired mother (and not using any quaint British swear words either). It took the whole hour to clean up, and then the kids were back and I hadn't even had a cup of coffee yet.

Clearly, I couldn't blame my lack of productivity solely on the kids. There was my own overtired condition and resulting stupidity. But my children did their part. They were not exactly obstacles to my work, because an obstacle is something you can perhaps overcome. They were semipermanent deterrents. No one told them to get in the way of my doing anything but taking care of their needs; it was completely instinctive. Like the age-old—or at least as old as the telephone—practice of interrupting mothers when they are on the telephone. This one made my mother laugh when she called and heard the kids dogging me, because I'd done it to her so many times for so many years.

They were at their worst when I had a business call. At first it was simply a matter of keeping my baby daughter busy and quiet. One time she sat on the kitchen floor and pulled all the strings off a box of fifty tea bags while I did a phone interview. I didn't stop her because it was such a quiet project. Then there were two of them, and soon they were older and actually seemed to enjoy ganging up on me. If I told them in advance to be good because it was business, they'd jump up and down as soon as I'd been connected with the interviewee.

"Can I talk? Can I talk?" If I tried to get away, it was worse. They'd chase me all over the place—"Mommy! Mommy! Mommy!" And if I locked myself in a room they banged on the door, screaming like I'd abandoned them. They fought; they got hurt; they needed to poop.

I resorted to putting my hands together and silently begging them to please, please let me finish the call in peace. This only led to their complete loss of respect for me as an authority figure, and then all hell would break loose.

The computer had the same type of draw as the phone. "Can I practice typing? Can I play Rodent's Revenge?" A little sticky finger would come up and press some key—I didn't know which one and they certainly didn't know—and my document would disappear or flush all the way left. I'm so computer illiterate I didn't know how to get it back. Or they'd click the mouse, or throw themselves into a piece of furniture and crack their heads or start screaming bloody murder, and I'd yell threats like, "I'm trying to work! Shut up! I'm going to beat you!" And then the neighbors would call child services. There really was no point trying to work while they were conscious. The kids, that is, not the neighbors or child services.

It was better that the children didn't know I had a career. The kids didn't want to know because it threatened their place as the center of the universe, theirs and mine. If I dared say, "Just let me do this few minutes of work . . ."

"But I don't want you to work!" would be the response, said with the same force and emotion as would the statement, "But I don't want to go to the orphanage!"

But when they watched *Bloopy's Buddies,* or *The Huggabug Club,* or *The Charlie Horse Music Pizza Show* or some other completely insane TV show and I sat with them, they wouldn't look at or talk to me for a full half hour. Or if I puttered around doing chores they ignored me—housework was acceptable to them. They liked to watch me iron, help me tidy and dust, load and unload the dishwasher, sort the laundry. But no moneymaking activities, please.

When the kids napped, I was in a race against time. I'd turn off the ringer and turn down the answering machine. I wouldn't turn on the computer because the tapping of the keyboard would wake them. They had bat hearing when it came to Mommy working, even while they slept.

"Mommy is not thinking about us. Wake up! Wake up! Revolt!" I sneaked around looking for writing paper, scribbling on the back of the mail. I had hidden the pens so my son wouldn't write on the furniture, but I never had one when I needed one. I couldn't check the kitchen drawer because it squeaked. There was a notebook in my bedroom, but they'd hear me in the hallway, so I ended up rifling through the coat pockets in the front closet for pen and paper and sitting on the floor by the front door trying to write with a leaky Bic on a supermarket flyer.

Needless to say, I didn't get too much done at any one time, a few pages at the best. So I wrote a lot at night once they were asleep, even though I was too tired and just wanted to channel surf and vegetate with my husband.

Some nights, however, the allure of Lucy, ice cream, and a comfy husband was too much, and I abandoned my chance to work. I figured I'd settle for working in short bursts until the kids were grown, when I'd be an old lady with nothing to do but eat bonbons and write. But then, of course, I'd want to be filling sippy cups and playing Rodent's Revenge and taking notes about it all in crayon on the back of an envelope.

8

---

bunk beds and movie stars

While we figured out where to live, with the kids getting bigger and the apartment getting smaller, I looked for ways to maximize our minimal space. The kids needed room to grow.

I went to the local children's furniture store to discuss bunk beds. I got to talking with the owner of the store.

"So tell me, which company does the best work?"

"We have no shoddy workmanship here. They are all quality companies."

"Sorry." He seemed a little offended.

"The price varies. What does your husband do?"

What does that have to do with bunk beds? "Actor," I said.

"He makes a living at that?" he asked, with an innocent look.

"Yeah, he does," I said. "Now, what's better—ash or pine?"

He'd already lost interest in the subject at hand. "I know someone who made a lot of money as an actress. You know her?"

"I don't know," I said. "Who is she?"

"She used to come into the store on Seventh Avenue. Before we came uptown. She's in the movies. What's her name?"

"Can you give me a hint?"

"Oh, I'll think of it when you've gone. She was in that movie . . ."

I raised my eyebrows and smiled. He made me ask. "Which movie?"

"You know the one. It was very . . . everyone was talking about it. How nice she looked in that movie."

"Do you know the name of the movie?"

"It was a very popular movie."

"What was it about?"

"It had that actor in it, you know?" I just stared. "He lives downtown . . ."

I took a guess. "Robert De Niro?"

"Yes, yes!" We were both excited now. "They made the film. She was very nice in it. She came into the shop all the time. Pat something?"

I was grasping at straws. "Blonde?"

"Yeah, blonde. Nice."

"Look, I have to go home now. But I'm sure it will come to

you. I bet it's on TV this week. You know how that always happens."

A salesman walked into the store. The owner said, "Remember down at the old shop, that girl who always came in. She was in movies. Remember? Pat something."

"Ellen Barkin?"

"That's it. Ellen Barkin. She did that nice movie."

So I guess we were talking about Ellen Barkin, not Pat something, and Al Pacino, not Robert De Niro. I suppose the movie was *Sea of Love*, but I'm still not sure. "She does well," he said. "Your husband should do movies."

"I'll tell him," I said.

"How old are your children?" he asked.

"Four and two."

He waved me out the door, "Too young for bunk beds! Come back in three years."

We'd have to find another way to make the kids' lives a little more free range and a little less veal calf.

9

impersonating home buyers

We decided to look at houses in the suburbs just to see what was out there. We chose a river town forty-five minutes out of the city in northern Westchester—not carefully, not after great thought and research. We chose it because some friends of ours had moved there and said it was nice. We visited their town a few times and liked it. They'd looked at other towns, and this one was the best. Mark and Lola said, it's great. That's the kind of research we conducted.

We thought we'd hit the jackpot when one of the first houses we looked at was a charming little cape on a great block at a great price. It was definitely within our price range, as our real estate agent put it, it was "the cheapest house in town." We decided to offer the asking price.

The owner accepted, and we were thrilled at how easy the process was. Until he called back and told our Realtor he'd decided to raise the price, claiming there was a bidding war. After great debates, we offered another five thousand dollars. After all, that still made it the cheapest house in town. Once again, we had an accepted offer. We were told we'd have to inspect the house right away.

I made a date to meet an engineer at the house a couple of days later. Lulu offered to babysit for a few hours if I hurried back before her waxing appointment. In the meantime my husband and I worked on talking ourselves into the big step we'd so hastily made.

So what if there weren't enough bedrooms or bathrooms and no dining room? We'd never had a dining room anyway. We decided either to keep the kids doubled up and all sleep on the main floor, or to have each of the kids in their own room downstairs while we slept upstairs. This would mean that, if they needed me in the middle of the night and I happened to hear them, I'd have to waddle (remember, I was extremely pregnant) down the stairs to the back of the house, around a corner, and through to the front of the house. The reverse (with an uphill climb) would get me back to bed. I'd also have to go downstairs for the bathroom. Not only did the second floor not have a bathroom, but, as I understand it, no one would agree to build one because it wouldn't be up to code without raising the roof. It's not legally a second floor. The ceiling's not high enough and the stairs aren't steep enough and on and on.

Otherwise, it seemed perfect. And what a price!

I showed up on a chilly gray day for the inspection, clutching a package of saltines and belting back ginger ale to quell my morning sickness. The inspector met the real estate agent and me outside. He'd already been up on the roof. After introductions were made, he put his hands on his hips and looked up. "Well," he said, without any particular emotion, "you're going to need a new roof." I wanted to crawl back to the train with my crackers and forget the rest of the inspection.

He explained that the roof tiles were peeling, there were already three layers on there, and we'd have to strip it all off and start over. "Like that one over there," he said, pointing to a house across the street. "See how nice that roof lies?" I knew nothing about roofs but was immediately jealous. Why wasn't that house for sale?

We went inside, where I was greeted by a strong smell of garlic. The babysitter watching the owners' children was roasting a chicken. It probably would have smelled great if I hadn't been nauseous, but for the next hour, I fought that chicken as it permeated every inch of the house. And every inch of me.

As we forged ahead, I got some good news. The house was generally well constructed. The sinks and tub drained efficiently. But during our inspection, the phone was ringing off the hook, and we could hear the answering machine messages as they came in. Numerous Realtors were leaving messages for the owner about coming to show the house. I turned to my real estate agent, "Do we have the house or not? This inspection is costing five hundred dollars, and that chicken is smothered in garlic."

She assured me that she would call the owner and tell him not to show it anymore, since he had accepted our offer. We went down to the basement to catch up with the inspector. He was looking at the boiler and the hot water heater. "These are shot," he said with a nod. So the bargain was going to cost thousands to fix up. It was becoming a fixer-upper, and we're not too handy. We backed out of the deal that night. Maybe it wasn't going to be so easy to find a house after all.

10

you start to live when you learn to drive

I traveled around the city powered by sneakers and a double stroller. My kids and I could cover forty blocks a day. That wasn't going to cut it in the 'burbs. We would need a car. Just the perfect added expense to tack on top of the potential house purchase that would probably break us.

I did some research and decided that the best car for our needs would be a minivan. We needed five seats just for ourselves, and what if a friend or my mom came with us? A station wagon had a lot of seats, but backseat passengers usually had to ride backward and that made us all nauseous.

I decided on the make and model and traveled to the dealership nearest our new house (even though we hadn't moved yet), so that once we did move, servicing the car would be a cinch.

I studied the ads, and my husband sent me off with strict instructions not to let anyone talk me into anything more than we could afford and to make them stick by the promises made in their newspaper ad.

I waddled up there on the train and took a cab to the dealership. Why was I in charge of this task? Because my husband doesn't drive. He doesn't like to fly either. He's basically not fond of transportation.

Now, some people consider this shocking, but it doesn't really faze me. Growing up in the city, lots of people didn't get driver's licenses. I took driver's ed in high school and failed my test and let it go until I was mocked into getting a license by friends in college. I called a driving school and took enough lessons until I could parallel park like a pro. Then I could stop bringing my passport every time we went to a bar.

My husband was never mocked, so he never got his license. It was never necessary.

Until now.

He promised that by the end of the four months we had left before this baby arrived, he would have a license.

So I was the one sent to pick out and test-drive the minivan. I emerged with a lease for about a hundred dollars more than we were supposed to spend, found out everything in the ads is a lie, and being pregnant gets you nowhere with car dealers. I was told I could get the car when convenient. Since we had no place to park it in the city, I decided to wait. Also, my sister was getting married in a few weeks, and I, as matron of honor, was throwing a shower for her, so things were busy enough.

The weather was beastly hot for June and very sticky the day of the shower. I'd booked the backroom of a neighborhood restaurant so I wouldn't have to do most of the work. Luckily, my sister's best friend from grammar school was cohosting the party, and she ran around in the heat gathering helium balloons and picking up flowers for the tables and cakes for dessert.

I picked up the kids from preschool, gave them lunch, and miraculously got them to nap. I felt fairly organized until I got the call from the Westchester car dealership saying I had to pick up the car I'd just leased.

"Today? I can't."

"Well, you don't have to pick up the car today, but you have to sign the contract and insurance. When can you be here?"

I reminded them that I didn't have a car. I couldn't get there that afternoon.

"We'll pick you up at the train station."

"I can't. I have kids. I'm giving my sister a bridal shower tonight."

"Okay. We'll bring the car to you."

This gave me pause. Having the car delivered and not making another train trip up to Westchester in this heat sounded good to me.

"The party is at six-thirty. How soon can you be here?"

"Give me until four-thirty," the salesman said.

I agreed, momentarily forgetting that I had no place to park the car.

My husband, the nondriver, soon arrived, looking like a wet noodle after running around the city all day, skipping lunch, and getting overheated. He went into the bedroom, turned on the air-conditioning, and collapsed.

I took advantage of the presence of a warm if not functioning body being home with the kids to run downstairs and tell the doorman, "If someone comes with a new car for me, make them wait."

"Oh, yeah, Mrs. Konig, a new car. They're going to give you a new car. Sure they are." I guess he thought the heat was getting to me.

"No, really, Alex. A man is coming to give me a new car. I leased it."

I set out for the garage down the street and stood sweating and haggling with the guys over a space for the next month. They finally agreed to an astronomical price.

I raced home, trying not to be frazzled about the impending party. I ironed my clothes and got my 4-year-old ready. She would come with me, and my husband and two-year-old would fend for themselves. If only the car would come.

My husband called from the bedroom, asking me to order some take-out food for dinner. "Can't you do it?" I asked, my voice rising to a frantic pitch. Just then the intercom rang. The car had arrived. It was ten minutes to six.

I ran downstairs and sat in the minivan with the dealer,

wondering how he had managed to put seventy-three miles on the car during a twenty-eight-mile trip. I madly signed papers without reading them as he told me, ". . . and these are your lights. Here's how you pop the hood. There are grocery bag anchors in the rear storage area."

I pushed him out of the car, peeled away from the curb, beeped at my doorman to show him I really did have a new car, and screeched around the corner into the garage. I tossed the key at the attendant and said, "Be careful, it's new." That was my first drive in my first-ever car.

Back home, I threw on my clothes, wishing I had time for another shower (though I'd showered an hour before), grabbed my daughter, and handed a take-out menu to my son, saying, "Give this to Daddy." The last thing I heard was my son saying, "Daddy, you have to feed me."

I made it to the party before most of the guests and had just started to relax when my husband called the restaurant and had me called to the phone. He had a developing migraine and could I please come back home and pick up our son. What could I do? One of the shower guests had already canceled with a migraine. It was that kind of a day. A migraine-inducing day.

I left the restaurant as appetizers were served, racewalked the four blocks home, grabbed my son, left my husband in a darkened room without pity, and returned to the party in time for entrées. The rest of the evening went pretty well, considering. I think my sister had a good time.

When we got home, my husband was on the mend. It was my turn to collapse.

The next day we took the car out for a family drive around Manhattan. It was then that I discovered that they had given me a model not only with no CD player but without even a tape player. It had no tilt wheel, no cruise control, no seat pockets for coloring books, and no roof rack!

My husband and I made some choice veiled comments about the dealership, but we were still excited to have a car. As we circled the city our daughter exclaimed, "This is the best day ever!"

11

---

a good old cat

"Do you think we'll love the baby as much as we love Scout?" This was the question my husband and I asked each other in the months before our first child was born in 1994. We were serious. We knew we loved our cat whether or not she was a mouser; we just had no clue what it would be like to be parents.

Needless to say, like billions of new parents before us, all our questions and doubts were answered instantly. We loved our baby. So did Scout, who slept beneath the crib every night, gritted her teeth and ran away when her fur was pulled, and, later on, lay on the floor and eventually let our toddler daughter rest her head on Scout's furry tummy. Eventually Scoutie lost some of the seniority she'd had for eight years and had to take a backseat to the baby.

On another night two years later we lay awake, again consumed in deep thoughts. Our daughter was now two (Scout was now ten) and in a few days the burgeoning population of our small apartment was almost certainly going to violate some city code. "Will we love the new baby as much as we love our little girl? After all, it's the three of us (well, four, counting Scout); how will this new stranger fit in?" Scout just lay on top of my huge belly and purred. She had already connected with the little stranger.

Our son was born, all twelve pounds of him. The morning I was scheduled to leave the hospital, the pediatrician came to me and said my son couldn't go just yet. He had jaundice and his bilirubin numbers had not improved enough for him to leave the hospital.

"But my 2-year-old is waiting for me. We've never been apart before." The doctor implied that the baby could probably be released that evening. So I reluctantly decided to go home to my firstborn. That night word came that my son would have to stay another night. It was the four of us now (well, five, counting Scout), and one of us wasn't home.

My daughter was watching *Dumbo,* and it was the part where the mother elephant is locked up in a cage and can't get to Dumbo so she sticks out her trunk and rocks him. I burst into tears over the little boy I'd carried for nine months and slept with in the hospital. We'd been attached all that time and now we'd spend the night with eleven city blocks between us.

It was a long night. The next day my husband brought our son home and finally we were all together. The new stranger fit in just fine. Scout waited patiently, purring. The moment both our babies were in bed, Scout fell asleep in my lap.

Now our daughter was four and our son was two. Scout was twelve. She developed kidney failure and started having seizures. We tried to hydrate her with fluids under her skin using needles and an IV bag in the kitchen every night. I never thought I'd be able to do anything like that, but I was a mom now. When her weight got down to almost nothing and she could only lie in the corner, we knew it was over. My son had just learned how to be gentle with her. He'd go over to her spot by the heater and pet her so softly and say, "Oh, key-kat." One night she wasn't in her place, and I feared the worst. She hadn't been able to walk more than ten steps without falling down. After looking all around, I found her lying like a proud sphinx in the middle of the kids' room. She was watching over them one last time.

12

---

the closing from hell

For a while things were quiet. We hadn't heard from either the building's rodent population or from our suburban real estate agent lately.

Luckily, it was our agent who checked in first. She didn't want us to get our hopes up, but there was a house and it seemed to have everything we wanted. We agreed to see it and—even though it was one of those houses that when you first see it, you tilt your head to one side and squint—within twenty-four hours, we were bidding on it, planning renovations, and losing sleep that the owners might actually accept our offer. They did.

I reinspected with the same guy. He must have thought

this was my hobby. This time no one was home cooking so there were no ambient smells. And there was no head-shaking at the roof or other major features.

The roof was new. So were the boiler and hot water heater. In fact the house had the Cadillac of boilers and hot water heaters. Finally some good news. The porch did dip to one side, causing an initial tilting/squinting reaction, but as the inspector put it, "It's been sinking for seventy years; it's not going anywhere today."

This four-bedroom bungalow with a stone fireplace, a nice yard, and a swing set seemed to have everything we needed.

The next thing we knew, contracts were drawn up. Then the lawyer called and asked, "Can you come sign on Tuesday, the thirteenth?" Novices that we were, we thought all handing over of money took place a few months down the line at the closing. "Do we have to bring any money?" I asked. "Just the down payment," said the lawyer. Oh, was that all?

So accounts were drained, savings bonds cashed in, the kids' room scoured for excess cash. That's not as strange as it sounds—we once found sixty bucks hidden in the Happy Meal toy bin. One morning I asked my two-year-old if he had a dollar for church. He reached into his pocket and pulled out a dollar . . . and a twenty. The boy had some kind of scam going on the side.

So we gathered our crumpled bills, three marbles, two jacks, and a piece of string and headed for the lawyer's office. By the end of the day, we owned 5 percent of our own house—which is 5 percent more than we've ever owned in our lives, and that's seventy-three years if you combined our ages. At least we owned it in theory; I think it stayed in escrow until the closing. At which point we owed the bank more money than the IRS had ever thought to hit us up for, and we'd been audited twice. But I thought it would be more fun paying down a mortgage than sending those tax checks off to Uncle Sam.

We had two months to raise the rest. All our owner friends promised that the closing would be the toughest part. "It will be the most hellish day of your life," they said. How bad could it be? We'd already met our attorney, a stranger, at a train station and given him all our money. Closing costs would be less than the down payment, and our mortgage company had given us a good-faith estimate. It's just a bunch of papers to sign, a few checks to be written, and we get the keys, right?

Well, not exactly. But we held on to this false sense of security until the day before the closing. I kept calling the mortgage company and going over the numbers. I was told the estimate was conservative, and they always make you bring more than you need. Our attorney agreed. If we had the recommended closing costs, we'd be sitting pretty with plenty of money left to live on and start painting and freshening up the house.

The day before the closing, we went up to Westchester for our walk-through. It was moving day for the owners, who were kind of stressed out but very nice, and we all sat on the porch and talked about garbage collection days, oil company contracts, and swing sets. The house was in good shape. We shook hands and my husband and I left, finally feeling like the house was really going to being ours.

That's when the closing costs hit the fan. Our attorney, the one from the train station, left the breakdown on our answering machine. There were two sets of numbers—a check for the owners and the actual closing costs. My husband listened and thought one was included in the other. With my perceptive reporter's attention to the matter, I understood that they were separate. The bottom line was that we needed three thousand dollars more than we'd been told.

It was 2:00 p.m. The closing was at 10:00 the next morning. The hellish nightmare was real.

The details of what followed are predictable. Cursing, swearing, tears, Tums, caffeine, phone calls, debts called in, understanding employers tracking down invoices and cutting checks, attorneys and mortgage companies blasted in vile terms, banks thankfully open late, dinner from the deli, everyone collapsing but nobody sleeping well.

Advice was given that we hold out at the closing and threaten to walk away from the whole deal or at least suggest we adjourn for thirty days. But the next morning there sat the owners, nice people who just wanted to get on a plane and fly across the country to their new home and job. My husband made a little speech, which succeeded in making everyone stare uncomfortably at their fingernails for about ten minutes. Our attorney said he understood that my husband was angry and needed to vent. "Angry? You think *this* is angry? Who's angry? If I was angry, you'd know it," my red-faced, forehead-vein-pulsating husband responded, as smoke literally poured from his ears. The owners smiled—they understood. Our attorney pointed out that the upsetting discrepancy was nobody's fault, then he blamed the mortgage company. I asked the woman representing the mortgage company if she had anything to say. "Look, I only attend closings; I have no idea what you're talking about."

In the end we signed the papers and wrote out the checks. The owners gave us the keys and said they hoped we'd be as happy in the house as they had been. We shook hands. I got teary. Our attorney took his check and fled.

We went to the new house and stood in the backyard and ate Drake's coffee cakes. It was over and we were now part of the American Dream.

13

leaving

I moved to the island of Manhattan in 1964 when I was two years old and my family was returning to America from France, where my dad had been working for a few years. We settled into an apartment on the Upper East Side, and I've never strayed far since. My husband came to Manhattan by way of Queens (his noble birthplace) and Da Bronx. Two city kids—and we were heading for the 'burbs. It would be a big adjustment (for starters, there was that driving hurdle for my husband). So as our big move to Westchester approached, we sat around bleary-eyed and stressed out in our half-packed apartment and mulled over what we'd miss—and what we wouldn't—as we traded in Central Park for the Saw Mill Parkway.

I'd miss the newly paved streets around our building on Lexington Avenue. I wouldn't miss the seemingly endless jackhammering and tar mashing that took place every night until 5:00 a.m. for four weeks.

I'd miss the sprinklers in the playgrounds from Central Park to Carl Schurz on the East River. For kids under five, there was no better way to spend a day. For overtired moms, planting ourselves on benches in the shade and watching the kids get soaked was a really good way to spend a whole summer. I wouldn't miss the organization—on a par with the invasion of Normandy—that it took for me to get my two kids out the door with bathing suits, towels, water shoes, buckets, bubbles, sidewalk chalk, crackers, juice boxes, apple slices, Pull-Ups, wipies—and a bottle of gin for Mommy (just kidding).

I'd miss being able to run down to the Korean grocers at 2:00 a.m. to buy a roll of aluminum foil and a quart of milk. I wouldn't miss spending eight dollars for a roll of aluminum foil and a quart of milk.

I'd miss my good neighbors in our building. I wouldn't miss the idiots who lived on Eighty-ninth between Lex and Third, whose garden backed up to our building and who threw loud, obnoxious parties on weeknights and disturbed people's sleep until the police had to be called as they boogied the night away celebrating Flag Day, Arbor Day, Grandparents Day, Gay Pride Day, Gay Shame Day, Saint Swithin's

Day, the Knicks winning, the Knicks losing, Julio Iglesias's birthday, and God knows what else.

I'd miss the cultural opportunities—museums, art galleries, street fairs, the theater, the opera—that abounded in the city. I wouldn't miss having to lie about the fact that I basically never took advantage of the cultural opportunities that abounded in the city. "Oh, is that Klimt retrospective closing? I'll have to put it on my calendar." And I did put it on my calendar, right next to "Don't forget to buy aluminum foil and a quart of milk."

I'd miss the apartment where I'd heard the pitter-patter of little children's feet for three years. I wouldn't miss the apartment where I'd also heard the pitter-patter of little mice feet for three years.

I'd miss my remarkable ten windows (so unusual for such a small apartment). I wouldn't miss throwing thousands of dollars in rent money out the very same windows every month (not unusual for such a small apartment).

I'd miss Lulu's unique take on life in the city and wished her well in her search for both the perfect rich, nonbalding, liberal husband and the equally important best sale price on designer shoes.

I'd miss raising my children as city kids. I wouldn't miss them running out onto the grass at our new house as they realized the swing set wasn't a public playground—it was their backyard.

14

---

moving day

My sister's June wedding had gone off without a hitch three days earlier. The baby was due in eight weeks. It was moving day. My husband had been packing boxes since the closing a few weeks earlier, and we seemed organized. We were labeling—kitchen, toys, books—we were neatly taping, we were inventorying. But when the big day came and the moving men arrived, we still weren't done. We began hurling stuff into boxes, quickly taping them up. The marker was misplaced, and the goal became to get out of that apartment. If we could have thrown stuff directly into the back of the truck we would have.

In the mayhem, I'd cleverly placed the running shoes I

wanted to wear that day not on my feet but on the shelf of the coat closet near the front door. When the movers came in with a wardrobe box, they grabbed everything in the closet and must have thrown the shoes in for good measure. When it came time to go, I had no shoes, none. My new seventy-dollar running shoes with the four-hundred-dollar orthotics were never seen again. I was barefoot and flatfooted.

My husband and the movers dug through the truck and found some sandals in a suitcase. When our apartment was empty, I walked with the kids over to my mother's apartment building. For three years we'd lived a block and a half away, and now her two grandchildren (plus an impending one) were moving to the far reaches of Westchester County—might as well have been Newfoundland. We lingered at the curb, took pictures, waved; we tried not to cry.

Then it was off to beat the truck to the house.

No problem. They took about an hour more than we did to make the forty-five-minute drive. We never quite figured out why. But once they arrived, they quickly unpacked, filling our bungalow with familiar things. Well, familiar boxes, anyway. They made five trips to the bathroom (one each, that is), accepted some cold drinks and a hefty tip, and were gone. I stood on the porch and started to cry. We were in our new house, our first real home.

My reverie was interrupted by my husband calling to me from the bathroom. The water in the toilet bowl was all the way up to the rim. "What do you think happened here?" he asked, reaching for the flusher handle.

"I don't know—*don't flush it.*" As the words came from my lips, and as if we lived in do-the-opposite-of-what-I-say-land, he flushed. The water cascaded over the rim, flooding the floor. We backed up in horror, and I heard more water, crashing and splashing somewhere below us. I ran down to the family room, where water was pouring through the ceiling tile onto my desk and boxed-up computer. I began frantically pulling stuff out of the way as my husband burst into the room and started screaming, "Get a mop! Get a mop! Go get a #*@!%@# mop!"

In tears (not of joy), I jumped in the minivan and went to the CVS. Once there my upset evolved into anger and I took my time, hoping he was suffering in our new home, willing the children to flush the toilet again so that it would splash again on the soaking carpet.

I compared mop-wringing mechanisms and prices. I browsed the plumbing declogger shelf, picked up a bottle of Liquid-Plumr. By the time I got back, my husband had enlisted the help of a neighbor with a plunger, and they were merrily joking about letting too many moving men use the bathroom. "Thanks for the mop, hon. Why don't you swing back to the store and get some beer for our helpful neighbor here?"

And so, the house christened, our idyllic life in the suburbs began.

15

cleaning for
the cleaning lady

Once we moved in, we decided that—with the new house, my perpetual state of pregnancy, and our soon-to-be three kids—we should hire someone to help with the house-cleaning.

My husband and I each had our own approach to house-keeping, and it was occasionally a source of friction. That's not exactly true—it was constantly a source of friction. We disagreed about what actually defined "clean." He believed "clean" to be an absence of dirt. I thought of it more as an absence of *visible* dirt. Yes, I was definitely a corner cutter, a sweep-it-under-the-rug, stick-it-in-a-drawer type.

And yet, my husband was neither Felix Unger–neat nor

Oscar Madison–messy; he was a little of both. He was the Odd Couple rolled into one–he was the Odd Single. He'd leave a pattern of coffee cup rings all over the dining table, but then he'd compulsively and noisily dustbust the baseboards. He never once put a diaper on straight over six years and three kids, but he'd go on fanatical laundry binges, stripping everything in the house and marching down to the laundry room. I mean everything. He'd strip down the shower curtain–while I was taking a shower.

I never got much sympathy from my girlfriends about this issue. The fact that my "life partner" knew what a "vacuum" was and could do a load of laundry while only irreversibly shrinking an average of one favorite cashmere sweater a year was cause for jealousy. It didn't matter if he was doing it wrong; it was that he was "doing it at all."

But he and I strongly agreed that we should get a little help with our new abode, at least in the short term.

Since I'd never had anyone else clean for me (except Mr. I-don't-understand-the-definition-of-dishwasher-safe-top-rack-only), I didn't know where to start or what to expect. So I put it off until, one day, I saw a troupe of six women entering my next-door neighbor's house armed with mops, pails, vacuums, and cleaning products.

"Each person takes a room and they do the whole house in an hour," my neighbor told me. "They'll even clean your fridge and organize your medicine chest."

"Wow." The search I'd put off had ended. I asked for the number.

When she handed me the slip of paper, her husband warned me, "Just get ready to clean before they get there."

"It's not cleaning," my neighbor said, "it's picking up. How can they clean if we don't pick up first?"

I arranged a precleaning appointment, a walk-through of the house by the owners of the service. Of course, I didn't want them to think we were a family of unrepentant slobs, so I tidied up before they came. So did my husband. And my kids. The entire family was mobilized into a frenzy of dusting and mopping and sweeping and sorting. The cleaners were coming.

When the screening committee showed up, the house looked okay, passable. I apologized for unpacked boxes in the corners of several rooms, left over from our move a few weeks earlier. I lurched ahead of the inspectors, picking up the odd block or action figure left behind in our quick sweep.

I heard myself promising that when they came to clean later that week, we'd have the place ready to be cleaned. They talked about clearing away the cobwebs from our ceilings. Gasp! It had never occurred to me to look up there. They must have thought we were savages.

A few mornings later the whole cleaning crew arrived. Of course the house had become a disaster area again, and we were dashing around "picking up." I rifled madly through the refrigerator, throwing away old meatballs and half-finished tuna sandwiches, not wanting the fridge to give the wrong impression about us. I was doing what I never do so that the people I was paying to do it wouldn't be grossed out.

I barked orders at my husband because, since I was too pregnant to bend and pick up all the junk on the floors, I was making him do it, and he wasn't doing it right. You never realize how much stuff is on the floor until a stranger vacuums.

Once the cleaning began, they took over and I had nowhere to hide.

I stood outside and watched through the glass doors. Two women were cleaning the family room and laughing and talking while they worked. I couldn't hear what they were saying so I tried to read their lips. I'm not that good at lip-reading, but I could swear they were saying something along the lines of, "Holy smokes, how can she live like this? Her inability to properly clean her own house makes us laugh. Ha ha ha!"

"I know, ha ha ha. This has to be the messiest house I've ever seen! This woman should live among the monkeys in some really messy part of the jungle because she is so messy. Ha ha ha!"

Whatever they were talking about, I know that I've never found anything quite so exhausting as the luxury of having a cleaning service.

16

too darn hot

In the summer months, domestic problems seem to find their source in the bedroom. You know what I mean, in the temperature department. As in, things heating up. Oh, all right, I'll spell it out.

It's the weather.

All marriages suffer when it's hot and sticky and raining a lot and there are mosquitoes and ticks and . . . When it comes to marital discord, it ain't the heat, it's the humidity.

Our first summer in the new house, after a mild July, we finally hit air-conditioning weather in earnest. Some like it hot—not my husband. Once the temperature rises above 68 degrees, he craves air-conditioning. Can't sleep without it.

Unfortunately, our bedroom AC was an old unit that emitted an alarming series of obnoxious squeaks, bleats, and rattles—sort of like a Stephen King novel where the appliances come to life and are trying to kill you. After a few hours of noisy tossing and turning, my husband reluctantly decided to switch to the open window/ceiling fan combination. But our windows stick so there was much grunting and heaving and accompanying mumbling that sounded something like @#$%&*! (just like in the funnies.)

The next thing I knew, he was standing in the middle of our bed reaching for the ceiling fan chain to adjust the fan speed, but he accidentally pulled the chain for the fan light. This light glowed with a Chernobyl-level brightness. In the middle of a dark night, it was like the flash from the A-bomb. He kept saying, "Sorry, sorry, sorry," but I was annoyed, having been marginally asleep through all this. He became annoyed with me because I was so cranky and insensitive to his climatically challenged condition.

After a while (a long while), things calmed down. Now he was sound asleep, and I was wide awake. During all the light and climate adjusting, he had found the time to go to the bathroom. When he came back to bed, he inexplicably closed the door to our room halfway. Now I never closed it at all because I was usually up with the kids at some point during the night. Later on this particular hellish night, one of our various children cried out, and I leapt from my bed to investigate. It was so dark I had my hands out in front of me, but unfortunately they went to either side of the door my husband had left ajar and I walked full force into the edge of the door. It was my face versus that door, and the door won.

"My face! My face!" I blurted. But I had a fat lip so it came out more like, "Muh faith! Muh faith!" My husband awoke gently, jumped a mile, and started yelling, "What? What happened? What's going on?" He was running around without purpose in the dark. By this point whichever child had been crying had gone back to sleep. Eventually, so did my husband. Me, I sat up with ice on my face and yearned for winter.

17

how to swim
and when to let go

Here's something good about the suburbs: the town pool. Mothers gather, children play, nice teenaged kids lifeguard. Much less hassle than the Y in the city. Join for the season and you're set. Snack bar provides a handy meal for nights you don't want to cook: "Sure, you guys can have hot dogs for dinner . . . again."

I was no *Baywatch* babe—for one thing, I was twenty-seven months pregnant. And I'd yet to master the art of emoting underwater for six minutes at a time without the benefit of oxygen while wearing a swimsuit that's three sizes too small.

But I knew a thing or two about swimming and water safety. I learned to swim well when I was about ten. My mother asked a lifeguard to teach me the crawl, breaststroke, how to dive, and how to tread water. That was the summer I really learned the rules that have stuck with me to this day. My husband's case was a little different. His dad took the "Old World" approach to teaching a kid to swim. When he was five years old, his dad threw him in a lake. This did not teach him how to swim. It taught him how to sink.

Me, I preferred the lecturing and demonstration method.

So I spent the remaining weeks of summer trying to impart this wisdom to my kids at the local pool.

My daughter took a class with other five-year-olds, and I let my son, who was pushing three, splash around at the water's edge. Though he couldn't swim, he wasn't afraid to put his face in the water—he liked going under and holding his breath. From under the two feet of clear pool water we were standing in, he looked up at me with his big blue eyes, which seemed to say, "Well, are you going to pull me up or not?" He was relaxed, as if it never crossed his mind that I wouldn't be there to save him before he needed air. His faith in me was very nice, but his Charley the Tuna imitation was shaving years off my life.

I threatened and bribed him (two things all the parenting books say never to do but which are, along with lying, my major tools as a mother). "Practice floating and you can go under again." I had seen a show where kids were taught that if they ever fell into water they should turn onto their backs and float. I wanted my son to learn this. "I'm afraid to float," he said.

The kid who spent half the morning under the water where there was no air was afraid to float on top of the water where the air was. "No floating, no going under the water!" I reprimanded and taunted him (I skipped that chapter in the parenting books, too). He sighed and turned his back to me. I supported him under his shoulders and told him he was sleeping on a bed of water and to relax. He was tense and kept bending his knees. I told him to put his chin to the sky, belly to the sky. "Okay, okay, let go," he said. Now he was getting irritated with me.

But he was too impatient and, as I let go, he bent in the middle, swallowed a little water and came up sputtering. "Now can I go under?"

I settled my girth at the foot of the lifeguard's chair by the water's edge while my son stood in knee-deep water repeatedly dunking his head below the surface. Each time he emerged, he had a shocked look on his face as if someone had thrown a bucket of water at him. He'd shake it off and then plunge back in again.

One time he came up for air, he lost his footing and fell completely under, flailing about as he went. I was an arm's-length away and reached for him. But the kid in the lifeguard's chair had already blown his whistle. He leapt into the pool with my son, lifted him from the water, and said, "Are you okay, little guy?"

This abrupt introduction startled my son, who began to cry. This was the same poor child I'd misplaced in Central Park.

I was trying to explain to the lifeguard that my son was okay, while telling my son that he was okay and that I'd been right there the whole time and saw the whole thing. Then I noticed them, like something truly *Baywatch*-esque. A dozen or so young people in lifeguard swimsuits, clutching those orange floaty things and running and splashing—seemingly in slow motion—toward us. I thought it was a drill or a group jog until they stopped where we stood in four inches of water.

It seems that once a whistle was blown, all lifeguards on duty had to respond to that area. "Is this all for my son?" I laughed nervously. "He's fine, you see." He whimpered, stunned over the arrival of so many people.

A young man with a black binder approached. "You'll have to fill out this incident report."

So the big pregnant lady is a bad mother. Too round and lazy to properly care for her toddler. I gathered my children and skulked off to get some fries.

Six more weeks of trying to keep his head above water and I could turn my attention to bike-riding safety. He'd get his first trike, first helmet. I could hear it already, "Okay, okay, Mommy, let go!"

18

---

the horrible truth about
bearing children

When another supermodel posed pregnant and naked on the cover of another magazine glorifying the shape of motherhood, the particular shape I saw was unfamiliar to me. I didn't even look like that when I wasn't pregnant. At four months I'd been about the same size as Cindy Crawford was at seven, but I looked a little, how do you say, droopy. When I stood in the same pose in the privacy of my own home, well . . . airbrushing would have helped.

By the time I was nine months pregnant I looked as though I had swallowed Cindy Crawford whole.

Looking good naked wasn't a priority. Simply appearing presentable out in public was a big goal.

I'd recently seen Cindy, clothed, on TV. She looked so pretty. I said to my husband, "Doesn't she look great?"

He said, "She's Cindy Crawford; she's supposed to."

"But she's about to have a baby."

"Oh."

But Cindy wasn't the only one looking good. I saw them out there every day just walking down the street. An abundance of women who go through pregnancy looking fabulous. And then there was me—the crazy sweatpants lady.

At least I'd escaped the city where pregnant women look fabulous. I mean, they look so good that they can make a nonpregnant woman feel downright dowdy.

In the suburbs many women manage to look quite stylish, but at least we have the option of hiding in our cars to avoid waddling past each other on the street.

Since I worked at home, I'd never invested in those great little work dresses that make pregnant women look so together. Those moms-to-be spent their days around other people and had incentive to appear presentable. I don't know why my poor husband didn't rate highly enough for me to put on something besides a really old plaid bathrobe with a mismatched belt from a preexisting old bathrobe. But he didn't.

I read those articles about choosing a few easy pieces—leggings, tunics, men's oversized shirts—how you don't have to buy a lot of maternity clothes. But every pregnancy the combination of being large, ungainly, and slightly off balance overwhelmed me. I felt like there was a reason they used to call it a period of "confinement." I should've been confined, the way I looked.

This largeness and lack of style was especially difficult as I was the daughter of a woman who practically lost weight while pregnant and always looked fantastic. "Oh, we weren't allowed to gain weight," said my mom. Well, that explains that! Hey, I didn't plan to gain fifty pounds with each kid. My metabolism conspired against me. As did Ben & Jerry.

"The doctor said that if I gained an ounce over fifteen pounds, he'd have me hospitalized," she said. Well, I could've stuck to a fifteen-pound gain if I had cocktails and cigarettes every night—pregnancy was much more fun in the sixties. My sister and I came out nice and small, and my mom went home in her own size-eight clothes.

But I had to face it. My mom and I were different people. She thrived on pregnancy. She craved oranges and Evian water. I craved pound cake and fried rice. She never felt sick and was her usual busy energetic self. I lay on the couch and threw up for four months. Then I stopped throwing up, but I stayed on the couch.

There's a picture of Mom taken literally moments after she gave birth to my sister. She looks gorgeous (my mother, not my sister—she looks like a little monkey). Mom's glowing, smiling, every hair in place, makeup perfectly applied, wearing one of those stylish bedjackets. My husband always says to her when he sees that picture, "You had just given birth?

My God, you look stunning! Amazing!" Then he turns to me and says, "Hey, honey, do you know your mom had just given birth in this picture? Isn't she something?"

Here's his subtext: "How come your mom looked this incredible and thirty-five years later, with all the advances in modern medicine, you looked like Shamu in drag?" I know what he's thinking. I gained what she gained plus one pound for every year that has passed since she gained them. The second time around I still had ten pounds on from the first baby so I was actually sixty pounds up. When I went into a restaurant, people would drop their forks.

My mom told about being whistled at when she was seven months pregnant. Her legs still looked nifty. Not only did my legs not look "nifty," my ankles had disappeared and my feet had gotten so fat I could only wear Velcro sandals. The only good part was that when I shaved my legs, on days when I had the energy to peer past my gigantic midsection, it was almost impossible to cut myself because there was no bone in sight. No ankles, no knees, no shinbones—just a wide plain of chubby puffiness.

I remember one evening right before my first son was born, I met Lulu for Mexican food and wore my groovy black maternity vest with the big silver zipper up the front. Though it had recently become a mite snug, I convinced myself that it was both slimming and fashionable. This delusion had added irony since Lulu often buys size two and then has the clothes tailored down to fit. When I sat down in the restaurant and the waiter had laboriously maneuvered the table back into place, Lulu looked nervous, as though she might have been injured by ricocheting zipper parts. "Isn't that kind of tight?" she asked.

"Shut up and eat," I said.

I was big. People were staring at me on the street, as if they all didn't get here the same way. Twins? Any day now? Triplets? One salcslady just started laughing and pointing when I walked up to the register.

"Is something funny?" I asked.

"Well, look at you! Shouldn't that be out by now?"

Not everyone was rude, but I started to get cranky. And the only thing that really fit me was a blue plaid tent of a dress, which can only be described as comfortable. I climbed into it and planted myself on a park bench when an older man sitting with a woman on the next bench leaned over and said, "I was just telling my wife you remind me of a painting by Vermeer sitting there."

"Don't you mean Rubens?" I snapped, imagining myself as a freakishly inflated caricature.

"No," he said, "we saw it on TV. A pregnant woman in blue standing in the light of a window with the sun on her hair. That's what you look like."

It was too late. I'd blown the gracious acceptance of the only compliment I'd gotten in weeks. Luckily for everyone, only days later I gave birth to a beautiful twelve-pound baby boy. He came out looking like an Irish cop.

This third time around I'd tried to keep my weight down, put an effort into what I wore, slapped on a little makeup and jewelry. I might not have ended up looking like a supermodel, but then again I wasn't appearing anywhere naked.

19

dead on the prairie

Right about now my mother would say, "Oh, for goodness' sake; you're making it all sound so awful." As usual, she'd be right. I am making it sound awful. Because it was.

In Lamaze class I saw all these warm and fuzzy videos shot through Vaseline of husbands and wives snuggling in these all-white, otherworldly birthing stations, sharing the woman's joyful labor. Or else the video would depict entire families relaxing on couches in a homelike place (if your home is decorated by Laura Ashley) awaiting the miracle with video cameras, soft music (think Yanni or John Tesh), and words of encouragement and declarations of love and support.

I got the no-frills special. First, I was in a labor room (which in fairness to the hospital might have had a little Laura Ashley wallpaper border up by the ceiling–frankly, I was in too much pain to notice). Then I was in an operating room. Then a recovery room. Then another hospital room. Then a taxi.

Giving birth, for me, was like being sawed in half, having a large, human being removed from my body, then being sewed back together again. As far as Kodak moments go, there's simply nothing else like it.

Our new baby would be my third cesarean. I was a three-time zipper case. I'd been told by many other women that I hadn't really experienced childbirth because I didn't deliver, you know, vaginally. That's another thing expectant mothers are forced to deal with–hearing the word "vaginally" from more people on more occasions than one ever could have imagined. Strangers on the street. Before–"What a pretty maternity dress! Are you going to deliver vaginally?" And after, "Oh, look at that cute baby! Did you deliver vaginally?"

I've also been told that doctors are very controlling, and that I probably didn't really need to have C-sections. If I had only let nature take its course, I could have experienced the miracle the natural way–without surgery, like the pioneer women. It's an interesting theory, but I think that if I were a pioneer woman, I'd be one thing–dead on the prairie.

I had my first two C-sections because I had two really big babies. By the time this third bundle came along, I had to be scheduled for a C-section. Any hard pushing and I would probably explode, that's what my doctor said. Actually, he used the word "rupture," but to me that meant explode.

My daughter came first. Fourteen hours of labor—it hurt a lot and I got very cranky and yelled at my husband when he said something helpful like, "Okay, you're having a contraction. . . ."

I was connected to about six machines and this was still at the noninvasive stage. They had a pulse monitor on my finger, a blood pressure cuff on my arm, a baby monitor on my tummy, an IV hookup for fluids, an epidural in my back, a monitor on the baby's head (she was still inside me—how'd they do that?), and a catheter to my bladder. For all I knew I might have also been hooked up to Strategic Air Command— one wrong move and we'd be bombing Cuba.

The doctor eventually told me the baby was nonreactive, which wasn't good. Natural shmatural. I immediately chose an emergency C-section, happily accepting all the anesthesia they could scare up at 4:00 a.m. I was perfectly willing to forgo my wonderful, womanly moment of femaledom to have a healthy child. My daughter came out great and weighed ten and a half pounds.

My mother, who had done it the old-fashioned way twice, told me, "You didn't miss much." And I believe my mother.

The second time around I was told, "This one is going to be big." Big. As in bigger than the first one. The doctor also said that large babies may suffer nerve damage if delivered, you know, vaginally. That was enough for me. I scheduled another C-section one week before the due date.

People have lots of suggestions when they find out you're scheduling a birth. Picking the date, for example. My sister made a big deal about picking my son's birthday. "What an awesome responsibility," she said. "You can pick his birthday. You'd better find out where the planets are going to be and what his sign will be and what time of day will make him an extrovert and . . ."

I called my obstetrician's office. His office manager (and wife) Mrs. Silverman said, "Dr. Silverman delivers on Fridays. How about the twenty-third?" So really it was Mrs. Silverman's awesome responsibility. I don't know what it meant astrologically speaking, but I had other things on my mind.

Friday afternoon we were all in the operating room, and they hooked up my epidural and I was ready to go and I heard this music. It had also been suggested that I might pick some significant and soothing music for my surgery, and it was on my list of things to do, but I forgot. Until I heard Heart's "Magic Man" coming over the operating room radio. This is not only a stupid song, but it's just about the worst music I could imagine giving birth to: "He's a magic ma-aan, yeaaaah, ohhhhh, he's got the magic hands, oh mama . . ."

So I sat up on the operating table and blurted, "I can't give birth to that." The doctors chuckled at my witty remark, pumped up my anesthesia, and went on with what they were doing. They weren't "controlling" me—they were ignoring me. Luckily the song ended and "Suite: Judy Blue Eyes" by Crosby, Stills & Nash started: "It's getting to the point, where I'm no fun anymore . . ." Not great but better than Heart. I was almost trampled during a Heart concert when I was sixteen. At least Crosby, Stills & Nash never physically endangered me.

Anyway, saw saw, pull pull, and I had a beautiful son. We cried. In a sterile operating room with stupid music playing, no Vaseline on the lens, no extended family watching from overstuffed sofas, it was still unbelievably wonderful. Not the birth part, just getting the baby into my arms. He was twelve pounds, one ounce, and a week early.

In an operating room three years later, on a Friday, our second son finally emerged during a commercial for an auto mall. Sad but true. He weighed only eight pounds, eight ounces. We almost threw him back. Instead, we took him home to our little house and to his sister and brother.

20

---

happiness is closet space

Since investing in the cleaning ladies twice a month, our house was cleaner but still disorganized. We had more closets than we could have dreamed of in the city, but they were already a mess. And my husband seemed agitated.

I found you can forget honesty. Forget communication. Forget having enough bail money to spring your spouse. The key to a happy marriage is . . . organized closet space.

Everywhere we've ever lived, he got the small closet, I got the big one. Why? I never throw anything out—what if those size-eight Calvins come back in style and I get my high school figure back? My closets always end up jammed floor to ceiling with wrinkled garments—which leaves me wearing the same five things over and over again because I can never find any-thing to wear.

My husband, on the other hand, likes to have all his shirts and sports jackets hanging neatly, all hangers (wooden—no more wire hangers, ever!) uniformly pointed in the same di-rection. But he'd never been able to maintain his perfect dream wardrobe because I'd always taken up all the closet space.

It's worse than Felix and Oscar . . . it was more like Joan Crawford and Oscar.

When we bought the house, we thought we'd finally have a place for everything. I took over the large closet in our bed-room, immediately crammed it full of clothes, and proceeded to wear the same five things all the time.

My husband took the walk-in up in the attic. It was all his, just his clothes.

Plus all the winter coats and everything I couldn't wear when I was pregnant and all the kids' Halloween costumes from the past five years were in that walk-in. It only took a few weeks to become a nesting ground for multiplying garbage bags of grown-out-of clothes, summer stuff, and maternity wear, as well as a catchall for empty boxes from new strollers and baby swings (what if we have to return them?). I also told Lulu I could store stuff for her—I wanted to show off how great the suburbs were because "there's so much room!" Not to mention numerous cartons full of old files, photos, and greeting cards I couldn't bring myself to part with.

When I started storing extra boxes of laundry detergent in

his closet, my husband put his foot down. He called a family meeting, like the dad on *The Brady Bunch* used to do, except I was the only one who showed up because our kids were too little to sit still and our baby didn't understand English yet. Either we fixed our closet problem or . . . he'd be really cranky and irritable.

We took the plunge. I remembered a recent magazine profile that described how Katie Couric had California Closets in her New York City apartment, and she seemed pretty organized. Perhaps this was the source of her perkiness! Well, if it was good enough for America's sweetheart, I figured it might help my troubled marriage.

I called California Closets and they sent over a lovely lady named Liz to take a look and find out what we needed. It was slightly traumatic to let a stranger see our closets. Her mere presence made me ashamed. Though she assured me that everyone's closets looked like mine, I ran ahead of her picking up shoes and tossing empty boxes into the hall. As she measured the spaces, I giggled nervously and said, "Ha, ha, what's this piece of junk doing in here? We don't need this!" and dramatically threw things over my shoulder.

A few days later the men came. They hammered, they sawed, they left. The result: I had, for the first time in my life, organized closet space. It included a long hanging compartment for evening wear (I planned to get some soon). I had sixteen shelves! I cleaned them. I lined them. I loved them. It had a velvet-lined jewelry drawer. No longer would my good jewelry be squirreled away in a cigar box at the back of my closet shelf where, every time I reached for it, a pair of ski boots fell on my head. And the convenient, easy-to-find drawer would keep thieves from ransacking our house while searching for valuables.

My husband got a network sitcom closet—you know, the kind that makes you wonder, "How come they don't have jobs but they live in a loft with such huge closets?" His included a velvet-lined drawer, too, for his one pair of cufflinks and his tie clip. He had a hankie drawer. He was happy.

Our closets were neat, and there was great joy in my house.

like a good neighbor,
we're fully insured

During our first months in suburbia, we lured our neighbors into a false sense of security—we convinced those poor, unsuspecting souls on our block that we were quiet, sedate, upstanding members of the community.

But suddenly, in one action-packed week, I narrowly missed crushing one neighbor's roof, and I succeeded in crushing another neighbor's car. Luckily, we had our new homeowner's and car insurance. The roof fiasco happened on the second of the month. The car fiasco happened seven days later. On the thirteenth of the month, my rates went up. It was quite a fortnight.

It all started with a rare tornado in Westchester. We had a

huge oak tree in our backyard, maybe six stories tall. I say "had" because the tornado sheared off about a third of it. It smashed through our fence and came to rest comfortably next door, on top of our neighbor's house.

The wind blew the huge tree limb straight down just as our next-door neighbor went out in the driveway to see if her car windows were closed. (They were.) She looked up to see the giant branch falling toward her house—specifically toward the bathroom where her teenage daughter was blow-drying her hair, getting ready for a date. Mom screamed, teenage daughter ran out to see what was the matter with Mom. Mom was relieved to find teenage daughter intact. Teenage daughter was irritated with Mom for screaming.

The fence between our properties, our tool shed, and an old dead cherry tree kept the branch from hitting our neighbor's house directly, and it was only the tippy branches that ended up sitting on their roof. No major damage to the house—although a soccer net was crushed and a guinea pig was scared out of its wits. Teenage daughter went off on her date—unscathed but with damp hair.

Friends encouraged us to file an insurance claim. "Just phone it in—you'll get a big check!" But others told me I might not get renewed if I filed too many small claims, and since I was newly insured, this might not be the only little disaster. Luckily, my husband and our neighbor were able to repair the damage together and saw up the tree for firewood and share relief that things turned out all right.

A mere seven days later, I was backing out of our driveway looking up at our broken tree, trying not to drive on my husband's new obsession, his beloved lawn, looking all around so as not to back over any small neighborhood children (or even big ones) when, suddenly, there was a loud crash as my car jerked to a halt. I had backed into my across-the-street neighbor's car, which was parked in my backing-up spot where she never parks (not that I'm trying to blame her; it's just that she never parks there, so I wasn't looking for her car as I was backing up because her car is never there; it's usually safely in her driveway. Honest, Officer . . .). Later I was to learn that this particular spot could be classified as a "blind spot." Nobody was hurt, but my kids were mortified. "Mom, you crashed into a car!" they helpfully observed.

I leapt out to examine her car, hoping that there would be no evidence. Unfortunately, the back part between the wheel and the bumper—which I would learn to call, in insurance repair terms, "the left rear quarter panel"—was pushed in and separated from the bumper.

I half parked my car in the middle of the street and frantically rang my neighbor's bell. She looked worried when she opened the door. "I backed up into your car."

She smiled weakly. "It's okay. Is there any damage?"

"I sort of moved something." She stopped smiling and came outside. I pointed to her quarter panel. She shook her head and said, "I never park here." I apologized a dozen times and told her I was insured. She said she'd get an estimate.

The estimate arrived on Monday. I'd put off calling my insurance company. Since the quarter panel was just a little out of whack, I thought maybe it would cost something like $200. That wouldn't be worth reporting, right? My estimate of the estimate was slightly off—by $1,100. I had dented her car to the tune of $1,354.08.

So I reluctantly called my insurance agent. I was embarrassed to be filing a claim so soon after taking out the policy. Did I look suspicious? Was I pulling some kind of scam? Was I deliberately crashing into my neighbors' cars? Was I deeply involved in a web of suburban–Barbara Stanwyck–*Double Indemnity* intrigue and deceit? My insurance agent chuckled sympathetically. Then he raised my rates 25 percent. Still it was good to be covered—it seemed to give our neighbors a little more confidence.

22

_____

can't shoot 'em

Since the baby came, we didn't get out much. So, for my birthday, my sister offered my husband and me the chance to go out to dinner, alone, together, to a restaurant, the kind where you make reservations and wear real shoes and make-up (me, not my husband). I was excited and called a little place I'd always wanted to try but hadn't been able to bring myself to make the reservation for any later than 7:00 p.m. After years of six o'clock dinners with the kids, we both get cranky if we don't eat early.

My sister arrived at 6:45, and I was happy to relinquish my overexcited brood. I told her what to feed them and to try to stick to their regular 8:00 bedtime. She shooed me away and ducked into the kitchen with the kids. There was much whispering and giggling and sounds of food preparation. Seasoned reporter that I am, I surmised there was some frantic last-minute birthday cake activity going on. They seemed to be baking it from scratch. Obviously the plan was for the kids to "surprise" me with the cake. But when? Seems my sister had not completely thought this plan out.

"So . . . you want us to come home while the kids are still awake?" I asked her.

"No, no, of course not. Go, have a great time." Then it hit her. "Oh, wait. Yes. Well—either you have to come home early for cake, or I have to keep the kids up late."

Her plan was growing more irritating by the second. "Okay. We're going out for dinner and you're going to keep the kids up late and pump them full of chocolate right before bed?"

"Hmm. Right. Okay, when do you have to be at the restaurant? In ten minutes? Hey, kids, come in the kitchen!"

There was much emergency cake decorating while my husband paced impatiently. "If I'm not sitting in front of a meal in the next twenty minutes, I'm going to get a migraine!" he offered helpfully.

Finally the cake emerged, "Happy Birthday" was hastily sung, and we were out the door.

Moments later we were at the restaurant. We got our menus, and I started to read the entrées and comment on them and look around at other tables and say how good everything looked and how I didn't know what to choose.

"Fifteen minutes to migraine," my date grumbled. The place was quiet midweek and the wait staff seemed to be hanging back, apparently not wanting to bother us so we could enjoy a nice conversation. They didn't know us very well.

We started to talk about our daughter's upcoming birthday. I said she wanted to have her friends over for games and cake in the backyard.

"We'd better get some more lawn furniture before that party."

"It's just kids. They can have a picnic on blankets."

"What about the parents?"

"It's just a drop-off party. Parents aren't staying."

"Well, I just don't think we have enough lawn furniture for this sort of thing."

"Whatever." I sighed.

"Where the hell is the waitress?" he muttered.

When you don't get out much, you forget how to pace yourself. The food arrived, and my husband and I engaged in a hurried frenzy of gastronomic overindulgence. It was not a pretty sight.

Ten minutes later we were really stuffed. It was now 8:15.

We decided to go somewhere else for coffee, just to make a real evening of it. But on the way my husband said, "Oh, let's just go home. I miss the kids."

When we got home, the kids were in bed but not asleep, and all hell broke loose because we'd spoiled their fun with their aunt and why were we home so early?

I drove my sister to the train and thanked her, telling her we'd do better next time. A newlywed herself, she shook her head over what had become of my husband and me. "There's chocolate cake in the fridge," she said.

I went home and my date and I ate cake in front of the TV and went to bed early.

23

nature stinks

Although we'd moved to a tame suburban street, there were occasionally aspects of Mutual of Omaha's *Wild Kingdom*. We knew, for example, that we had a skunk, and, at first, it seemed exotic. Then it just smelled.

The skunk came with the house, although no one mentioned it at the closing. It meandered through our yard nearly every night, merrily leaving its scent along the way.

One night was particularly pungent. Our noses woke us up. "Mom-may! What is that smell?" My daughter seemed to blame me for not controlling the situation. Though none of our windows were open, the odor wafted in through the old wooden frames. I guess it was my fault we hadn't ordered re-placement windows yet.

I improved the air quality with a can of Glade Neutralizer and went back to bed, grumbling about the wretched beastie who'd awakened me when I already had four other people in the house who could manage that just fine.

By morning the smell had usually faded, except after the night the skunk hid under our minivan and I opened the door and nearly passed out and we had to ride to school with the windows open and I wished I had one of those little pine tree deodorizers hanging from my rearview mirror.

Before this pungent experience, I didn't know much about skunks. There was that cute one in *Bambi*. And I remembered that episode of *The Partridge Family* when the skunk got on the bus and the Partridges had to go to a hotel and order about six-thousand tiny glasses of tomato juice to bathe in. As a child, I remember thinking, "Why didn't room service just send up the large cans of juice? They're not going to drink it." I also worried about the hotel bill, already knowing at a young age how hotels overcharge for tiny glasses of juice. It would be years before I understood the value of a sight gag.

So that's what I knew about skunks.

Until one night when my husband and I were watching TV in the family room, and we looked out our patio door and there it was with its little skunky front paws up on the glass looking in at us. My husband ran to a switch on the wall. "I'm going to flip on the outside lights and startle it!" I explained to him that there might be a serious downside to startling a skunk, so instead we waited for it to waddle away.

We shared our skunk with a neighbor. After the furry menace strolled up our driveway, it crossed the street. Our neighbor had an actual face-to-face encounter with the skunk while taking out the garbage. As he walked outside one night, his motion-activated outdoor lights went on and there was the skunk. They looked at each other, and the skunk raised its tail, and . . . nothing. "Westchester skunks are lazy," said my neighbor. "A warning was all he could manage."

But if they don't spray out of fear, does that mean that skunks are smelly when they're just walking around? Do they stink up the neighborhood for fun?

I was told there are things I could plant around the yard that skunks don't like. Mothballs, for instance. I was giving this a try one day when our house painters, local guys, complained of the lingering odor on our property. I asked their advice. "You need to get a Havahart trap," one guy told me. "You know, the kind that doesn't hurt them." That sounded like a plan.

"But then what do you do with it?" I asked.

"Oh, then you drown 'em."

I didn't ask my painters for much animal-control advice after that. This skunk was a pain in the nose, but it was here first. I just kept hoping it would find a place it liked better—somewhere far away from us and far away from any house painters who think wildlife is submersible.

24

---

suburban peril

The kind of helpful though bizarre advice dispensed by our house painters was par for the course in our new community. Up here, instead of minding their own business like folks in the city, neighbors watched out for neighbors and everybody knew what everybody else was up to.

This had its advantages. For instance, it was quite safe for little Girl Scouts to go door-to-door (with their moms or dads) and sell cookies. The only danger here was overconsumption. Until we moved to Westchester, we'd never had the opportunity to buy Girl Scout cookies. We didn't know any Girl Scouts. So when my husband learned that he could purchase

Thin Mints from the comfort of his own home and have them delivered in a few short weeks, he was ecstatic.

When the cookies arrived, he ate three boxes in thirty-six hours. He was sick. And he wasn't the only one. Women in our neighborhood were complaining that their dopey husbands were eating too many cookies. And it showed. Most of the dads on our block had that "too many Thin Mints" look. It was the secret shame of the modern suburban man.

Then there was a scandal. It didn't involve the Girl Scouts, but it might have been triggered by all those cookie boxes in our trash. Our quiet street was visited by mammoth, wild, grizzly type bears and simultaneously residents' garbage started to disappear mysteriously. I'm no theologian but I believe this could be the first sign of the oncoming apocalypse.

All right, they weren't grizzlies, but there were a couple of reports of black bears being sighted around the town. Then, coincidentally (or was it?), full-to-the-brim trash cans were being stolen without a trace. The incidents made our local paper's police blotter column.

Our neighbors were among the first to be victimized. These were not the neighbors upon whose house our tree fell, almost killing their guinea pig. And they're not the neighbors into whose parked car I crashed, causing thirteen hundred bucks in damages. These were the plunger-lending, skunk-sharing friends.

In spite of their generous assistance on key plumbing occasions, we'd shared no major disasters with these neighbors yet. That is, until their garbage was stolen. Not just the garbage but the cans containing the garbage. All of it: cans, trash, nothing left at the curb.

Who takes garbage? The bear, right? But their garbage wasn't eaten or spilled out all over the street. It was stolen, in the middle of the night. When they came out in the morning, everyone else's garbage was sitting there ready to be picked up, but their two cans, full of garbage, had vanished.

The plot thickened. Murphy, the dog next door, was heard barking on the night in question at an unfamiliar car parked on our street. Not a truck. A smallish sedan. Could this have been the getaway car of the notorious garbage thief? But where do you put two full cans of garbage in a smallish sedan? The trunk? Wouldn't fit. Inside the car, horizontally? Remember, this was not the perpetrator's own garbage, about which he or she would know where it'd been and who had chewed on it. This was stealing someone else's garbage. Who would want that all over their backseat?

The next day our neighbors thought they spotted their missing garbage—in our driveway. One of our beige Rubbermaid drip-proof waste-removal containers looked very similar to their own. The police were called, and, this being Westchester, they actually showed up to investigate. Of course, since we were conveniently away for the day, I momentarily became the prime suspect in the case.

The police looked around our yard to make sure nothing was amiss. Nothing was. I thought I was in the clear, but you never know—maybe the police thought I was only pretending to be away from the house but was actually hiding inside waiting for the perfect opportunity to abscond with more of our neighbor's garbage.

The whole thing was baffling. Was someone looking for old credit-card slips? These days you can lift that kind of information off the Internet from the comfort of your own home without touching anyone else's yucky trash.

And I know that if I throw out a sales receipt, I rip it in half and throw old soggy cereal and used tea bags on top of it just to make sure no one's going to be charging up a storm using my good name.

Meanwhile, no one on our block was sleeping. They were all staying up and peeking through the blinds to see something: a quiet thief with a big car, a new and inexperienced garbageman who picked up from a single house and didn't know you don't take the cans with the trash, or a really tidy and determined bear with strong paws.

The cans never reappeared, nor did the bears. We finally ran out of Girl Scout cookies and things were calm for a while.

25

the ex-pets

The kids wanted a new pet. Their little brother had been around for a few months and the novelty had worn off. They wanted something furry, with four legs and a tail. Excuses were hard to come by now that we lived in the suburbs. We had the room; we had a yard; we had a minivan. A domesticated beast of some kind was the next logical step.

But before we got a new pet, a young pet, a pet that was alive, we had to deal with old pets, the ones that were no longer with us, *les*—as the French say—*animaux morts de maison.*

One night at bedtime, our five-year-old started thinking about our old cat Scout, who'd died about a year earlier. She got very sad reminiscing about her old feline friend, and I tried to cheer her up by talking about getting a new pet. But she didn't want that. She wanted Scout to come back to life.

I told her Scout was in heaven.

"But where's her body?"

"Well, she's not in her body anymore."

"Did you bury her?"

"Well . . . we never had a place to bury her before we bought this house."

"Do you have her body?"

"Um, they do this thing with pets where they turn their bodies into ashes."

"So where is she?"

"In a special box."

"Where's the special box?" There was no getting around it. She was obviously determined to pursue this line of questioning all the way to the end. I had no choice but to fall back on that last resort of parenthood—I told her the truth. "In my closet." On one of my sixteen shelves.

That admitted, we planned a nice burial ceremony out back.

"But what if we move?"

"We will never move. Good night."

Hopefully she wouldn't make the connection that, to date, everything I'd attempted to bury in our backyard (daffodils, tulip bulbs) had been dug up and eaten by squirrels.

I'd mentioned that my childhood dogs were also "made into" ashes and put in special boxes. She wanted to know where they were.

"Pop-Pop has them." I was sure my father had them, and I was pretty sure he'd never gotten around to burying them.

So I asked Pop-Pop. "The dogs? Oh, they're in my nightstand." Good Lord, he slept next to them.

I told him my daughter was afraid that we'd move after we buried the cat.

"Then bury Scout at my house." There's an idea. Or we could just put her in the nightstand.

Since we were talking dead pets, I told him that when I was in Central Park one day there was a lot of excavation going on around the bridle path near the reservoir. "You know," I said, "where you buried Myrtle."

I was seven years old when I won that turtle at Melissa Groo's birthday party and, after it lived its short, happy life, my father was dispatched to find a nice final resting place. Ever since, I'd visited this same spot in Central Park with fond turtle memories. My husband challenged the truth of the story: "I'll bet your dad just told you he buried that turtle."

Nuh-uh. My dad wouldn't do that. Would he? I asked him, "What happened to Myrtle?"

"Do you want the truth?" Not really. "I threw Myrtle down the incinerator chute."

The man's a monster. What a way to go.

Then there was Mr. Manders. On my fourth-grade camping trip, I found this adorable little salamander named Mr. Manders and I brought him back to the city in a coffee can full of grass, leaves, and twigs. I figured he could live in my room.

My room was also my sister's room, and she was less than thrilled with this idea—so my dad offered to find Mr. Manders a nice home on Long Island. He claimed to have released Mr. Manders in a damp woods on the North Shore. When I asked him about it, he said, "If I said I did, then I guess I did." Very reassuring.

If we did get a pet, Pop-Pop was not going to be on the short list of pet sitters. Clearly, this strain of pathological dishonesty ran in our pathologically dishonest family.

26

---

a new cat

One night I was telling the kids a story about a cat that got lost but managed to find its family on the other side of the country. Our daughter started to cry.

"I'll never see Scoutie again." My husband and I did our best to comfort her with hugs and lots of great stories about cats romping in heaven. We gave her cookies. She was inconsolable. We brought up the idea of possibly getting another cat. This time it worked. By bedtime, her crying over, she said, "I'm going to dream about my new kitten."

When we saw the ad in the paper for a cat adoption day, we piled in the minivan. Not wanting to get the kids overexcited and possibly disappoint them, we spoke in code and pig latin all the way to the mall. "What if there aren't enough *items* to choose from?" asked my husband.

"They said on the phone that they have a lot of *items* every weekend." "How much will the *item* set us back?"

"They ive-gay it to you, but you have to pay a all-smay ee-fay."

"A small fee for what?" asked our multilingual daughter.

When we got to the mall, my husband pretended to go to Office Depot, but he was really checking the pet store to make sure they had kittens for adoption. He came back to the car. "Let's go look for a pet."

Our daughter giggled with happiness while our son did the "Oh yes" dance, which is kind of like the conga. The baby chewed on his sock.

Inside the store we approached the pet adoption area set up by volunteers. One lady was holding a tiny kitten and petting it. My husband, who had already told this woman we were looking to adopt, said, "This lady has a kitten for adoption." But another woman blocked our way, saying, "Oh, I didn't know you had all these small children. Perhaps you'd like to see our older cats. Small children might hurt a kitten this small. We don't feel comfortable letting you adopt a young kitten."

She gestured at the baby. "You really have to keep an eye on little ones like him."

"Yeah," I said, "because ordinarily we don't watch him at all."

My husband got his really angry expression on his face so

I quickly ushered our daughter over to some cages to see who was inside. Lots of older cats, some youngish cats, and only three kittens. Two were black and white and there was a tiny white one hidden behind them with green eyes and a little pink nose.

"Mommy, look at the little white one with the gray on her head," said my daughter. "Can I hold her?"

I hesitated because I knew she'd want the first one she held. I turned to another volunteer and said, "Is there a point in letting my daughter hold that kitten, or are we going to be rejected as inappropriate?"

She opened the cage.

The kitten put her nose on my daughter's nose and licked it. "She kissed me!" said our delighted daughter and new cat owner.

"What's her name?" our son wanted to know.

"Snowball," said his sister.

Snowball came home and we fixed up a nice basket with a blanket and a stuffed cat in a warm spot in our daughter's room. Snowball proceeded to spend the night in our bed jumping from my head to my husband's, purring loudly and pouncing and swatting at our earlobes.

We didn't sleep much, but our daughter didn't stop smiling for a week.

27

fill 'er up

The thing about being New York City apartment dwellers our whole lives—doorman buildings, walk-ups, nice apartments, dumps—we took certain things for granted. Like heat and where it came from. That was always something "they" took care of, as in, "Why don't they send up more heat?"

After we moved to the 'burbs, we were responsible for our own heat. "They" were now us.

In the fall, when the first cool nights arrived, we were afraid to turn on the heat because we thought we might blow up the whole house. Since we'd moved in during the summer, we'd never thought to ask the previous owners how to work the thermostats. It turned out this wasn't just a simple matter of flipping an on/off switch—our thermostats were state-of-the-art, space-age, intimidating little computers. They could be set to all sorts of creative combinations like 70 degrees at night until half past midnight and then 68 until 6:30 a.m., automatically adjusting to a slightly toastier 69 for the day, except on Sunday when it should be 71 around the clock. The oil guy came over and carefully examined the apparatuses, considered them thoughtfully, and rendered his professional judgment—he didn't know how to set them either. He said just hit the "up" arrow when you want it to be hotter and the "down" arrow when you want it to be cooler.

Some like it hot. My husband liked it really, really warm. (I know, Mr. I-need-air-conditioning-in-summer goes completely the other way in winter. It may be a mineral imbalance or something. Maybe God is just testing me.) As a homeowner I thought he'd be the "put on a sweater" type. Our old apartment had had so much heat that the issue had never come up before. But at the house, he kept hitting that "up" button to 74 every time he passed the thermostat, and I'd walk by and click it down to 70. Everyone I knew was beefing about the price of oil that year—I figured 74 had to cost more than 70.

Besides, it was too darn hot.

Close to Christmastime, I finally found a gauge on the oil tank in our basement, and it looked low. It was kind of hard to read, but it appeared to be less than one-eighth of a tank. I called the oil company, and they said they'd fill us up the following Monday and that it was unlikely we'd run out completely before then.

About 6:00 Sunday morning, I woke up cold. I knew immediately what was happening. I checked the kids—they were tucked in pretty well. The temperature in the house was fast approaching the lower 50s. I brought the baby into bed with us and elbowed my husband awake. "Hey, are you cold?"

"Yeah," he innocently responded. "Why is it so cold?"

"BECAUSE WE'RE OUT OF HEATING OIL!"

He took my helpful suggestion to get on the phone with the oil company immediately and tell them we had a newborn and small kids in the house.

We had a full tank within forty-five minutes, for a slight emergency surcharge ($75).

Later that week, we invited our favorite couple from across the street—the ones with the stolen garbage and the plunger, who'd helped us with the overflowing toilet the day we moved in—to join us for some holiday cheer. They diplomatically asked what was going on the Sunday morning the oil truck came. After all, who orders oil on a Sunday? "We ran out of oil," I told them. They asked at what temperature we kept the heat. My husband told them he liked to keep it at 74.

"No," came the sage voice-of-experience reply, "that's too high. You can't go above seventy." Suddenly, like the conversion of Saul, this now seemed like a great idea to my husband. Of course, when I had said the exact same thing to him several times, I'd gotten a lecture along the lines of, "We didn't buy this house so I should be cold all the time! If a man wants to walk around his own house in the dead of winter in shirtsleeves, then blah blah blahbity blah!"

Everyone in our part of the state claimed never to have paid more than 99 cents a gallon for home heating oil—until we moved there. The last time we filled up, we'd paid over two dollars. And we just burn it up with every cozy night's sleep and every warm bath. We considered taking out a second mortgage on the house to fill up the oil tank. Instead my husband took to chopping firewood for our lovely stone hearth with a vengeance. After all, there was all that timber from the tree-falling fiasco. He broke two axes, but it kept him warmed up and out of the house.

28

a stomach flu
for the new millennium

The horror began when my three-year-old son woke up with it. For twenty-four hours he was in preschool purgatory and then, thankfully, got all better in that bounce-back way kids do. We made a big fuss over the poor little guy since the illness is pretty violent and can knock a kid on his knees. The teachers at school were talking about it. Seems this strain of the stomach flu was tearing through the neighborhood faster than a gangsta rapper throwing loaded guns out of an SUV. We'd been pretty lucky that it hadn't spread through our whole house.

Our luck lasted until one morning at 3:00 o'clock, when the experimental tacos I'd made for dinner came back to haunt me. It was an especially poor choice for a meal right before this thing hit. By the time daylight rolled around, I was an empty shell of my former self. If Social Services had come to the door and said, "Let's see you take care of your kids today," I would have had to throw up my hands and say, "Take 'em! Don't get me wrong, they've been great, but stick a fork in me 'cause I'm done." Luckily, instead of Social Services, our babysitter showed up and my husband took the day off. He was extremely helpful, standing over my limp body saying things like, "Boy, are you pale. You're white as a sheet." A regular Marcus Welby.

That night, aside from that pervasive run-over-by-a-steamroller sensation, I was feeling as though the worst was over. By the next morning I had a sneaking suspicion I might actually live, and I began to get all our lives back on track. For instance, in two days, I was expecting twenty-five people at my house to celebrate my newborn son's christening. I had to think about things like marsala and ziti and shrimp—in large quantities. At least it didn't involve tacos.

I was getting organized. It didn't last long. By later that night, in the wee small hours, my husband and our five-year-old daughter simultaneously succumbed to the Wes Craven movie that was the winter's stomach flu, and it was a revolving bathroom all night long with Cinderella (yours truly) hauling sheets and changing pj's and chasing everyone with a bottle of Fantastik. The apocalypse continued through the next day until the patients basically passed out from exhaustion.

Me, I had a stir-crazy three-year-old and an infant and 265 loads of laundry and two sinks of dishes and hands that felt like sandpaper because I had to keep washing them every time I touched anyone or anything in our house. And I still felt like a squeezed-out rag from my own bout with the flu.

I decided to postpone the christening. Even if everyone got better within the next twenty-four hours, this little bug was obviously highly contagious, and I could just imagine twenty-five relatives spending a few hours in my hot little house and taking home the gift of severe illness.

I sneaked out to the Dairy Mart for apple juice, ginger ale, and saltines and ran into the Realtor who'd sold us our house. She was in a full-length mink coat and heels. I was in the red flannel shirt I'd slept in, leggings, Wellington boots, and my husband's parka—all topped off with some seriously unwashed hair. I looked how I felt—lousy. "You look fabulous!" she beamed. "I love that look!"

Apparently dehydration and an oily scalp become me.

a martha stewart-less christmas

It was Christmastime and, attempting to be the perfect mother, I tried to make sugar cookies from scratch. Instead of turning this holiday activity into a Kodak moment, I nearly had a nervous breakdown.

My daughter's school sent a notice announcing the big Christmas pageant and party with a blank space to indicate what homemade treat I'd be bringing. At least we were given the opportunity to come up with our own contribution—for the Thanksgiving party I'd been *assigned* corn on the cob. Corn on the cob! And I had to cook it that morning and bring it in hot! I'm still getting over it. My friend Debbie only had to bring apples. Not peeled, not sliced. Just apples. Didn't even have to wash the pesticides off 'em. This time I wasn't going to get stuck boiling vegetables in bulk, so I said I'd bring cookies.

What a quaint family holiday endeavor! Me, in the kitchen with my daughter, baking Christmas cookies. Just thinking about it made me giddy.

It took me two days to shop for all the ingredients: flour, sugar, brown sugar, butter, baking powder, vanilla, eggs, and chocolate chips—more groceries than I usually buy in a week, it seemed. Cookies are supposed to be an express-lane purchase, a prepared food, an open-the-box-and-serve dessert.

I also had to buy nuts because I'd bragged to my friend Debbie (with the apples) that I was going to make cookies from scratch, and when she suggested nuts I said, "Sure! Nuts! Why not?" I was bound and determined to meet any and all cookie-related challenges. But then I remembered that my kids don't like nuts and the school always sends out warnings about nut allergies, so I ate them all before I even began baking.

Ready for a Norman Rockwell baking experience, I called my daughter to the kitchen with a cheery, "Cookie time!" I measured each ingredient and let her pour it into the bowl and stir. Within moments I became concerned about spills, nervous that my three-year-old son would run in and touch the stove, irritated by bits of eggshell in the batter. I got a little distracted and put in, well, not enough flour. The recipe called for two and a quarter cups and I only put in one cup. I probably don't need to mention that this is kind of a vital ingredient. As we spooned the cookies onto the cookie sheet, they did feel a little mushy. Once in the oven, the cookies immediately ran off the cookie sheet and dripped all over the place. My daughter was shocked by my incompetence and immediately lost interest in the whole project.

The next morning I went to the supermarket, bought a roll of slice-and-bake cookies, and shoved it in the oven. Then I sat down on the couch and watched TV. In eight minutes, I had three dozen perfect sugar cookies with a snowman design in the middle, and my daughter thought I was really cool. The cookies were a big hit at kindergarten, although one show-off brought risotto.

So I decided not to get too intense about Christmas. For example, I had envisioned the whole family picking out the Christmas tree—all four of us walking arm in arm to the tree lot, my husband puffing cheerily on a pipe (he doesn't smoke a pipe, but I was going to suggest he take it up for the occasion). After all, back in the city, buying a tree is just a trip to the Korean deli, where they're propped up against parking meters. This was to be our first country yuletide season.

But when the time came, the baby was napping and my other son was cranky. I considered dragging them all out—half asleep, ill-humored, and all—and forcing them to judge tree quality against their wills. I caught myself. Adjusting my plans, I sent my husband and daughter on the mission, and as it turned out, they picked out *the* best tree in town. The kids decorated it by putting about fifty ornaments on one low branch and—a new trend—socks and hair ribbons strewn on like garlands.

The baby woke up, looked at this mess of a tree, and smiled.

*

30

a big irish ma'am

I'm driving down the road with the music blaring. I'm wearing my shades, the Bee Gees are playing, and I'm singing along, transported back to 1978: "Night fever, night fev-uh, you don't have to huh-huh." Didn't know the words back then either, but I was sixteen and dreaming of a day when I'd be on my own, making my own decisions, living the life.

Well, as it turns out, I'm a grown-up cool chick, and I've got my own set of wheels. I pull up to the minimart to buy a Tab—just one calorie to keep the disco momento going. I hop out of the car and saunter past a group of teenage boys, locals hanging out front. They size me up and I wonder if they think I'm some new college girl who just moved to the area.

Inside, some construction guys are picking up their lunches, ordering sandwiches. One holds the door for me. I say thanks, and he smiles. Those hard hat guys always like the ladies. They can see I'm a free spirit.

I choose my refreshing beverage and put exact change on the counter. I'm too busy and popular to wait on line. I head for the door and remember to ask for a straw. The kid behind the counter making sandwiches hands me one and says, "Here you go, ma'am."

The needle scratches off the LP that's been playing in my head.

Ma'am? Ma'am? Since this isn't the Old West, I'll take that to mean "old."

I turn slowly to the door. Everything has stopped and no one's made a move to open it. This time I catch my reflection in the glass. It's like getting smacked in the head with the cupboard door that you opened but forgot to close when you bent over and then you came back up. Where's the cool chick from the car?

The poor broad I'm looking at has got to be at least thirty-eight years old, seriously droopy from the recent birth of her third child, and her "set of wheels" is a seven-seater powder blue minivan with three car seats and a lot of Cheerios on the floor. She's sporting the extra-extra large denim shirt she bought three babies ago and the telltale baggy sweatpants of a suburban housewife who's having a fat day.

Still, ma'am? What about miss? I know I'm married, but miss implies youth. Ma'ams need help crossing the street.

I flashed back to a recent Sunday when we were leaving church. I'd felt a tug on my sleeve. A little girl about six looked up at me and said, "Mrs. Konig, my dog is harmless."

Who was this and what did she mean? After a moment of feeling eerily frightened, I realized it was simply a girl from my daughter's class who wanted a play date and felt she had to convince me that, if my child went to play at her house, her basset hound Oscar would not be a problem.

"Okay," I said. I thought the sentiment was cute, but was mostly taken aback by her calling me "Mrs. Konig." No one ever called me that.

When I was little, I called all my friends' parents Mr. or Mrs. or Dr. So-and-so. But somehow that seemed overly formal coming from my children's friends. I wasn't sure I wanted them calling me Mrs. Konig. But when three or four-year-olds called me "Susan," hearing my first name from the mouths of babes was kind of jarring, too.

My children had their own solution for what to call their elders. They'd name them according to their relationship to their children—Olivia's mommy, Trevor and Ruby's daddy, Emma's babysitter. But these adults often corrected them and told the kids it was okay to call them by their first names.

The children were so comfortable with this arrangement that when I told them to call a good family friend Aunt Lisa or Uncle Jim, they dropped the "aunt" and "uncle" and it was just Lisa and Jim. Teachers at school, however, remained Mrs. Tramaglini, Miss Ladd, Mr. Gallagher.

I guess it's a generational issue. I saw the father of one of my grammar school friends over the holidays, and he told me to call him Arthur. Arthur? I'd called this man by his surname for over thirty years. I tried but I got all nervous and couldn't say it. The best I could do was shorten his name to Mr. C.

Then I met a friend's mother who was in town and I asked what I should call her. Her grandson was calling her "Gaga Lily." That's what she told me to call her. I suddenly felt more comfortable calling her "Travis's grandma."

My husband's been calling my mother by her first name since the day our first child was born. I was doing a little involuntary convulsing after an emergency C-section and lots of anesthesia, and my mother got a little weak in the knees from the sight of me. My husband caught her in his arms, and since then they've been on a first-name basis.

He still calls my father Mr. Brady after almost ten years of being his son-in-law. My father hasn't corrected him, but once wrote him a note and signed it "Pop-Pop," which was what my kids call him. I wasn't sure my husband wanted to use that handle. Maybe if my dad felt a little faint.

Back at the Dairy Mart, one of the teen hooligans pulled the door open and held it for me. Reality set in, the movie of my life got rolling again, but there was no music. I smiled weakly. "Thank you."

"Don't mention it, ma'am." There it was again. I winced and waddled away. I hoisted myself back into my car and turned the key with a sigh. The radio was still turned all the way up and now it was Perry Como singing "Besame Mucho." It turned out to be an oldies station. In the blink of a bloodshot eye, the songs of my youth and Mr. Relaxation were now in the same category as I . . . a part of ancient history.

It was time to go home to my husband and the kids. He'd had them alone for a whole twenty minutes, and I was sure it was getting to him.

"Hey," he said, "how was your big break?" He was glad to see me. He assumed I was refreshed and ready to resume full-time motherhood. The kids were bringing him his paper and a snack on the couch. Next he'd have them doing our taxes.

I shrugged and settled my girth into the rocking chair by the fire. "I am old and fat," I announced.

My husband usually called me his "big Irish wife." But on this day, he saw I was down and said, "You looked nineteen when I met you and you still look nineteen." That made me feel better. After all, whom did I need to impress—my husband or the hooligans at the minimart parking lot?

My husband, of course. Still, I kind of wish the hooligans thought that I'd borrowed the van from my mom.

collectibles and mershicals:
the scourge of
modern christmas

"I want that! Mommy, can I have that? Mommy, do you see?"

For the twelfth time in as many minutes, I glanced up at the TV and told my kids, "Put it on the list."

It had been this way for a few weeks since the Christmas barrage of toy commercials began. They didn't even watch that much TV, but an hour of Nickelodeon meant about twenty-five commercials, or "mershicals" as my son called them.

And it started all of a sudden, like a chemical reaction. They wanted every single toy they saw on TV. Correction:

My daughter wanted every single "girl" toy, and she thought her brother should have every single "boy" toy.

If boys were playing with something on TV, she didn't want it. "Mommy, I don't want that. That's a boy toy."

But her brother saw what she wanted. Every time a Barbie mershical came on, he reverently said, "Wow."

I told them both to make a list of everything they wanted and then when it came time to write to Santa, they could pick three or four items off the list that they really, really wanted.

My daughter concocted a pretty good list for a five-year-old. Her handwriting was neat, and her spelling was close enough to get the idea. She also included her brother's requests since all he could do was draw a lot of squiggly lines on paper, pretending he was writing. The baby was on his own.

Here are some of the things they wanted:

Magic Stroller Baby
Hungry Hungry Hippo
Chicken Croquet
Crocodile Dentist
Hoppin Boppin Space Ball
Sparkle Fairy Barbie, Blooming Barbie, Flying Barbie
Barbie's Dream House, Barbie's store, Barbie's vet office
Barbie's dentist office, Barbie's little sister who pees
And Mr. Bucket

If that wasn't enough, there was one more holiday gift obstacle to overcome. It was the insidious poison endangering schoolchildren across the country—the trendy toy of the season.

Yes, there'd been the horror that was the great Tickle Me Elmo shortage followed by the regrettable Furby mania.

Furbies were those little furry dolls that could learn English and talk back to you and sneeze, and if you didn't properly care for them they could die. How delightful.

There had been a picture in the newspaper of the foul object that season. "I want that!" my daughter cried.

"You don't even know what that is," I said.

"Yes, I do. It's a . . . a . . ."

"It's a owl!" my son proclaimed.

"It's a bird," she agreed, "and it flaps its eyes at you."

"Flap your eyes," I told my son.

He happily blinked his eyelids and flapped his arms up and down for good measure.

"See," I told my daughter, "your brother can flap his eyes and his arms and he doesn't cost seventy-nine ninety-five."

This year, the trend came in a little foil package at about five bucks a pop. Those darn Yu-Gi-Oh and Pokemon trading cards. Kids were buying up carloads of the stuff in order to get a rare card so they could then turn around and resell them to collectors at a huge markup, thus turning the kids into rabid compulsive gamblers (what a racket!). "White eyes, Blue eyes dragon!" they'd yell.

What was wrong with parents spending all their money

on useless pieces of cardboard? Wouldn't it be a lot simpler to turn to their kids at some point and say, "No," as in, "No, you cannot have thousands of dollars to buy Pokemon cards; now get upstairs and clean up your room!"?

Pokemon fights were breaking out in schools. Bullies were taking Yu-Gi-Oh cards from smaller kids. Teachers banned the cards. This continued a fine, American tradition of banning trading cards at school. I remember when Partridge Family cards were banned at my school. We'd spend a lot of time trading for cute pictures of David Cassidy and it became distracting, so the nuns said, "Enough!" But we were just crazed preteens. There was no money involved—a pack of Partridge Family cards probably cost a quarter. And you got gum.

Our kids got some Pokemon cards at a birthday party and found out that everyone wanted them, so they traded them back and forth. Our daughter cheated her brother out of his because he didn't know any better. Then I found the precious cards underneath the seats of the car. For all I knew there was probably a "rare" one down there mixed in with stale Cheerios, empty juice boxes, and a sock or two.

The good thing with my kids so far was that I could put my foot down, and then basically get by until the trend passed without too much heartache. I'd refused to purchase any video games, handheld or otherwise, having seen kids zone out so completely that, if they lived in a cartoon, they would never notice that anvil falling out of that building. And in the 'burbs, the new rage was having video game systems installed in your minivan. I was bucking that fad by forcing the kids to play "I spy with my little eye . . ." and "twenty questions" on long trips.

Unfortunately, I knew about video game addiction and it wasn't pretty. When I was first married, I had an assignment to write about a kid's video game called "Sonic the Hedgehog." I needed to see how it worked so the company sent me a system to attach to the TV. I got the gist, although I wasn't very good at it, and I was constantly letting that hedgehog fall into the abyss to get hit with nunchucks or some such horrible fate.

But I did my work and then forgot about the system connected to my television until I found my husband sitting zombielike on the couch at 4:00 a.m., playing the game and trying to get to the next level. "Must achieve Emerald Zone," he chanted. To save my marriage, I had to box the thing and send it back. The game, that is, not my husband.

Luckily, the kids accepted the Christmas guidelines fairly well and even came up with some gems of their own. My daughter told me, "I really want a new ball." She'd lost hers to a buck-toothed raccoon who'd popped it one night in the backyard—it was one of those $1.69 kick balls from the variety store. "I'll share it with my brothers," she promised.

We could handle that.

32

---

let it snow

It seemed as though it used to snow a lot more when I was a kid than it does now. Except for the winter of 1993–94, when I was expecting my first child while pounding the pavement apartment hunting in Brooklyn and we had seventeen snow-storms, it just didn't snow that much anymore.

And as a curmudgeonly home-owning adult, I was glad about the lack of seasonal accumulation. Frosty the Snowman was no longer my snowy childhood friend, delighting me with the magic of winter. He was evil. I had a minivan and no garage. Snow just meant lots of scraping and defrosting of windshields. Santa could keep it; I wasn't interested.

Except when we got our first real snow in the new house.

It was supposed to start during the night, so, when I was up at 4:00 a.m. to check on the baby, I peeked out to see if anything was going on. Nothing. I was a little disappointed because I'd thought it would be fun for my kids to wake up and see the yard all covered in white.

But as the whole family began to stir around 7:00, sure enough, it began to snow in earnest, big old flakes. My son and daughter ran to the window and started jumping up and down in their fleecy longjohns. "It's snowing!"

I was glad for them, could almost remember being that way when I was little. After all, my sister and I put in long hours on the Seventy-ninth Street Hill in Central Park, bombing down the slope and crashing through drifts until we were frozen. We'd rush home and change and try to convince our mom to let us go out and do it all over again.

But now I worried about the roads and how much would fall or stick and whether we were responsible for shoveling the sidewalk in front of our house. We were.

We got a two-inch coverage–just enough to look nice and not be too much of a nuisance. The school bus came on schedule, but my daughter had me out there ten minutes early so she could try to catch snow on her tongue and examine the flakes' individual patterns before they melted in her gloved hand.

When she came home with two of her schoolmates, the snow had just started coming down again. Joined by her little brother, my daughter and her friends marched straight to the backyard without debundling or asking for a snack or if they could watch TV. In their scarves, gloves, and parkas they looked like snow-crazed mini–Michelin men. They threw themselves down on the ground, madly flapping their various limbs to make snow angels. They tossed the powdery snow in poofy handfuls at each other. They tried building a snow-man, but the snow was too dry to stick to itself. Gloves came off and the bare-handed method was attempted. Too cold. I was summoned to warm eight hands.

Our little piece of the pie was less than a fifth of an acre and the yard was relatively flat. But at one side, it had a hill. Well, an incline. Let's say the terrain undulated a little. For three five-year-olds and a three-year-old, that was plenty. I grabbed the Flexible Flyer and called out, "Who wants to go sledding?" The cheers, the accolades, I was a hero.

I showed them how to sit one behind the other and where to rest their feet and the screaming and thrills began. Riding down that little droop in our lawn looked like the most fun thing they'd ever done. There was much debate over who went next and who sat with whom, but they stayed out there until they had worn away all the snow in our yard and the grass showed through again.

Then, despite subarctic temperatures, the paper-thin coating of white stuff pretty much melted away. But for a few hours, I was reminded of what snow was all about aside from shoveling and scraping and defrosting.

33

the baby's surgery

When our baby son was cleared for surgery, I lost it. I didn't lose it right there in the pediatrician's office. I waited twenty-four hours and picked a huge fight with my husband over cold cuts. There were none in the house and apparently it was my fault. I got in the car, went to the deli, bought the cold cuts, and then threw them at my husband. Big fight. Remember Ali and Frazier and the "Thrilla in Manila"? This was the Grief over Corned Beef.

I was scared because our ten-month-old had to have an operation under general anesthesia. He'd been born with a common urological condition that could be easily fixed with a relatively short surgical procedure. Simple, common, no big deal—and completely nerve-racking.

We were supposed to be at the hospital, a fifteen-minute drive from our house, by 8:30 a.m. My wonderful sister and her equally wonderful husband had come up from the city the night before to help with our two older kids. I set the alarm so we'd have plenty of time to consume coffee and fight over the newspapers before we got in the car.

When the alarm went off, I felt drained and exhausted, as if I hadn't slept at all. After showers, coffee, pointing my brother-in-law down the hill to the train station, we finally said our cheery good-byes. The baby was strapped in, bottle bag and stroller loaded up, and we were on our way.

We got to the corner and my husband said, "Now what time do we have to be there?"

I told him, again, 8:30. "Then why does the clock say six fifty-nine?"

I'd set our alarm clock an hour ahead by accident the night before. Even though every other clock in the house was set on the right time, in my addled state I had somehow assumed that they were all wrong and our alarm clock was right. We turned the car around, went back to the house, and groggily killed another hour. Then we said our good-byes all over again and hit the road for the second time.

In our family we'd had good experiences with hospitals and bad ones. Luckily, this one was good across the board. From the moment we walked in, everyone was terrific. Every receptionist, every nurse, every doctor and resident. Even the guy who made coffee in the cafeteria. Compassionate man, needs a better blend.

They took us to the OR. I had to put on a paper jumpsuit and booties and a shower cap and mask. Our tiny guy was wearing a little green hospital gown and standing in his rolling crib charming everybody. They attached a pulse monitor to his toe and a blood pressure cuff to his arm. Then they put an anesthesia mask over his face. As he fought against it, I told him it wasn't my idea and kissed his shoulder. A nurse walked me out with an arm around me, and I made it back to my husband without crying. I'd determined not to cry at all because once I start, I'm completely useless.

A little over an hour later, the surgeon himself came to get us with a smile on his face. Everything was okay. He took us to recovery, where our son was sleeping. My husband and I took turns holding him for hours. The kid's a real trouper. By six o'clock he was home, sleeping in his own crib.

We counted our blessings. The clocks were all set on the right time, there were plenty of cold cuts in the fridge, and the baby was fine.

34

the sewer comes to us

The kids were asleep. My husband was out at a union meeting. I had the whole evening ahead of me with a pint of Ben & Jerry's Chocolate Fudge Brownie Low Fat Frozen Yogurt and complete control of the remote. I skipped happily downstairs to the family room, but my good cheer was cut short from the feeling and sound of my foot squishing into the basement carpet. It didn't just squish, it splashed. The room was flooded.

I reluctantly put aside my dessert and looked at the door that led to the unfinished part of the basement. I didn't want to know about the source of the water. I knew that there wasn't a big wave of water waiting behind the door like on TV, but I knew it wasn't going to be good or simple.

We'd had water in the back of the basement for a few days. Every time we went to do laundry, the floor would be wet. We'd put down some newspapers, inspected all the pipes and spigots, but couldn't figure it out. Then we'd pick up the papers, but a few hours later, the floor was wet once again— even if we weren't using the washer.

Unscientifically, we decided that there'd been so much snow in recent weeks that the ground couldn't absorb the moisture so it was seeping slowly through our normally dry basement walls. For some reason we liked this explanation, and felt we could keep sopping up water until the snow went away.

Unfortunately, this theory was shot to hell when I opened the door to see, not only a full inch of water covering the whole concrete floor and slowly seeping through the dry wall onto the family room carpeting, but to find my slop sink completely full to the brim with oozing brown muck.

For no particular reason, I decided the gunk might overflow (clear water I could deal with but not brown sludge) and so I plunged my hands down to the drain to make sure there was nothing blocking it.

When I was up to my elbows, I realized that this liquid was raw sewage. And it was coming in from the drain and that it wasn't going to go away. Wimpering like a girl in high heels being chased by a swamp monster in a horror film, I wiped my hands on some newspaper and ran upstairs to disinfect my limbs.

It was 9:30 at night, so I did the only logical thing—I panicked and called my neighbors. Yes, the plunger and home-heating-oil-advice neighbors.

"There's a backup in my sink," I said.

"Oh, do you need a plunger?" she said.

"I don't know. I think it's sewage."

She told me she'd send her husband over to take a look. The poor man started bailing the stuff and carrying it out into the dark and the snow of my backyard to dump it. After a few trips, we noticed that the level wasn't going down. In fact, whenever any gunk was removed, the sink filled back up to the brim.

"I think the sewer's backing up into your house," he said. "Did you look in that bathroom?"

He was pointing to a door right next to my washer and dryer that led to a defunct bathroom that we were told could be functional with a little work but that we'd decided to leave alone and had, in fact, completely forgotten about.

"But that bathroom is all dry. Nothing works." There wasn't even a light fixture. The room was long and narrow and kind of spooky. The toilet was on a concrete platform, to be above the sewer line, I'd been told. Using his flashlight, my neighbor showed me that the sink and the toilet were also completely filled to the brim with sewage. Next to the toilet, through a bolt in the concrete, clear water was bubbling up and probably had been for days, the source of the clear water on the floor.

There must be a blockage out in the street, he said, and this must be the lowest point on the block so here's where it's coming in.

Just our luck. Out of thirty houses, the lowest point is a bathroom in our house we don't even use.

That night I found out that all the twenty-four-hour plumbers listed in the *Yellow Pages* are lying. No one could or would come out to help me that night. One guy agreed to come in the morning and told me not to flush or use any water in the house until he took a look. Always an easy trick with five people living in a house. I closed the door to the Gateway to Hell and squished up the stairs to bed.

By morning, miraculously, the sewage had receded, leaving a serious ring around the slop sink. The plumber said it was because no one on the block had used their water overnight. But the previous evening, as everyone bathed and flushed and got ready for bed, the whole sewer system was sliming into our home. He called the town and got an emergency team working out in the street with a Super Rooter Machine. "There was a blockage, all right," the foreman told me. Could have been a tree root, accumulated garbage.

Meanwhile my house started to smell. I foolishly tried to clean up by renting one of those sucking, shampooing, drying machines that restores carpets like new. But after an hour of pushing that thing around, I realized that the underpad was also soaked and was actually disintegrating.

I marched down to the Town Hall, placed the smallest of my children on the counter, and began complaining about health risks and lack of sleep and the inability to work in my home office, which was in the family room.

They were sympathetic and offered to pay for the plumber and the vacuum rental. I asked them about new carpeting. "Well, your old carpeting won't be appraised for anything near what new carpeting will cost. And you'll be getting a new room out of the deal."

"But I don't want a new room. I liked the family room the way it was. Your sewer backed up into it."

"Well, we're not going to say that it's our fault. Maybe your homeowner's insurance will pay for it."

Here's what I learned. The insurance company will only pay for sewer damage if you have sewer-damage coverage.

I went home and ordered the carpeting I wanted from the first guy who said he could do it that week. With a scarf tied around my face, I cut up the ruined carpet with a box cutter and threw the whole mess out into the snow. My husband took over the disinfecting-the-floor part. The installer took away the old carpeting for an extra fifty bucks. I tacked that on to the convenience check I wrote him.

After much arguing, faxing of bills, and throwing one insurance adjuster out of my house, I finally got about 70 percent of my expenses back. I was too tired to fight for more.

The water works supervisor called me and finally told me they'd removed a huge tree root from the sewer pipe out in the street.

We painted the room peach, and it looked quite pretty. We scrubbed the Gateway to Hell room, closed the door, and went back to pretending it wasn't even there.

35

---

who's watching the kids?

The girls next door were finally getting old enough to babysit. They were thirteen. But they were twins, so together they were twenty-six. And their parents were home.

We'd missed the opportunity with their older sister, who was already into sports and being social by the time we moved in. Except for the time our tree fell on her house, she was rarely home. We would take advantage of this sliver of teenage-dom when young girls think babysitting is neat, and they don't have a million commitments yet.

Their mom told us the twins were interested in doing some sitting, and I was thrilled. Not that we went out very much, but it was nice to have the option and they could come some afternoons if I had a deadline and keep the kids busy.

I needed help. I couldn't watch the children all by myself all the time. But it wasn't always that way.

After our first child was born, our daughter, I felt that only I could care for her. No one else could provide for her adequately, including my husband, who would beg me to go get some rest. "No, what if she needs me?" I even slept with her strapped to me in a baby Snugli for a while.

Then I became the baby. That's right. At night, when I was falling asleep, I had these kind of out-of-body experiences in which I would feel I had become the baby. The only thing I can compare it to is the sensation you get when you've bodysurfed in the waves all day, then lie down at night and close your eyes and you still feel the motion of the ocean. Well, I'd close my eyes and feel the baby's feelings and mannerisms as she slept in her crib. Weird, huh? So my husband didn't have a chance.

Eventually, reluctantly, I learned to trust him, along with my sister and my mother. But that was it.

I spent the first year keeping the baby to myself. New mothers often seek each other out in the park to compare notes or just to talk to another grown-up. I discouraged such conversations. I'd fuss over their children and then say, "Well, I have to go over there now." And I'd find a quiet spot to stare at and talk to my baby. We'd go to the playground, and I wanted to play exclusively with her.

Needless to say, this special time did nothing for helping

me separate from my baby. She was fifteen months, and I'd never left her with a babysitter. At the time, we lived in a brownstone in Brooklyn, and our landlords would often offer to watch her. They were a charming Italian couple, always sending up a bowl of gnocchi, a plate of cannolis, inviting us into their home on holidays, giving us flowers from their garden. They had grandchildren of their own and were retired with lots of time to spare. They were the ideal babysitters, ideal, right out of central casting, heaven sent. I never took them up on it. They were just too nice.

Finally, after a year and a half of no sleep, no dates, no breaks, we needed a vacation, so we took a cruise (a writing assignment, a great deal). It was a dream come true. The one-room cabin was compact but comfortable—big bed, two comfy chairs, a TV. The staff had set up a cozy crib in a walk-in closet. They took out all the shelves, put in a tiny refrigerator for milk and juice bottles, and placed a curtain across the door. It was just perfect for our daughter, who went right off to sleep every night, lulled by the rocking of the ship on the Atlantic.

There was even a babysitting service on board that arranged for a member of the crew to sit in your cabin at night. Well, we had to admit, it seemed like a legit operation, and how far could someone get with your kid while on a ship at sea? Dolly, a small, kind-faced woman from the Philippines, arrived and listened patiently as I told her every idiosyncrasy of our sound-asleep child and showed her where the bottles were and told her what "baba" meant should my child call out, "Baba, Mama." Dolly, the mother of four, knew what "baba" meant. My husband literally shoved me out the door, and we were off to the casino. We called about ten times and didn't stay out long, but it was a nice break, and Dolly just sat in an armchair eating our fruit basket and watching movies on TV while our daughter slept soundly without a single request for a "baba" or "Mama."

The next night, emboldened by my success, we decided to do dinner, dancing, the whole business. But we didn't get Dolly. We got Audrey who, when we left, was standing in the closet over the baby's crib watching her sleep. We pointed out the comfy chair, the TV, and what was left of the fruit basket, but she waved us off. After dinner my husband stopped by the cabin (another advantage of being on a ship) to check on the baby. She was fine, asleep. But the babysitter was still in the closet, perched now on top of the tiny refrigerator. She sat there with her hands folded in her lap. When I checked in an hour later, she was still there—on top of the fridge, staring at our baby. I told her she could go in the bedroom and make herself comfortable. "No," she said, "I was hired to watch your baby, and that is what I am going to do." We finally called it a night because I just couldn't have a good time while this woman was sitting in a dark closet on top of a cold refrigerator staring at my baby.

The next night I called and begged them to send Dolly back. I mean, there's overprotective, and there's creepy.

After our romantic getaway, I was predictably pregnant once more. We left our brownstone and moved into the apartment building in the city to be closer to my mother. It's funny how the thought of having two babies at home suddenly makes you want your mother.

There we found Emily, the teenage babysitter everyone in our building hired. Of course, I didn't rush into anything. We'd heard lots of good reports about Emily from the other parents, and then spent months getting to know her on the elevator. I could see she was a great kid, natural, loved spending time with her parents (hello!), no weird rock 'n' roll friends. And her mother was a doctor and liked to check in with Emily personally while she was babysitting and bring her a little dinner.

Everything seemed to check out, and it had been a long time since Audrey the refrigerator-sitter, so I got up the nerve and asked Emily to sit for our daughter about a week before our son was born. We figured once we had two kids, we'd really never go out anymore even though we already didn't go out anymore. I was thirty-four years old at the time and pushing two hundred pounds, but for some reason I assumed this sixteen-year-old would see me as a slightly older, cool version of herself. She told me what high school she attended, and I said, "Oh, I took Driver's Ed there." "Gee," she chirped back at me, "I didn't know that program had been around that long. I mean that it's that old." Okay, so she didn't envision me as slightly older or cool, but she *was* a good babysitter.

I was lucky that my family lived in the same city, but they were busy with their own lives. If I did leave the kids with a sitter, I fixed the food because only I knew how they liked it.

Too much mayo on the tuna, and there'd be a revolt. I bathed them (really not to be left to strangers) and got them ready for bed. I exhausted myself.

I called a million times to make sure everything was all right. If it was in the afternoon and I came home early, I felt I should take advantage of the babysitter's presence and get stuff done, but there we all were in my small two-bedroom apartment. So I decided to go out and do the grocery shopping, and I was schlepping all this stuff thinking, maybe I should get a housekeeper because she's up there playing with my kids and I'm doing all the boring stuff.

A mom once said to me, "We're looking for someone not just to watch them but to love them, to be a member of the family, to be motherly." And I said, "Gee, how about you? You're a perfect biological match."

And how to decide what to pay? If someone came really cheap, I'd think, "Great, I found a bargain," and then I'd remember it was to watch my kids, and I'd wonder why they weren't charging the fortune I'd pay to keep my children safe. And if they charged too much, I'd think, "I'm sorry, it's not worth it to me to pay that much to keep my most precious possessions out of harm's . . . oh, never mind."

Toward the end of my second pregnancy and through the six weeks of recovery from a C-section, I was forced to hire someone to help me with my daughter, to get her out and run her around a little. We got Shirley, who had cared for two of my elderly relatives over a period of years. Shirley was not only a registered nurse but had been an auxiliary police officer. She was rather imposing physically and quite capable of taking charge of a situation. She even had two young grandsons living in her house in Canarsie and was an expert in baby care. Still, various members of my family felt the need to follow Shirley around as she took my kids out. It could be that my kids were the first of their generation to be born so they were somewhat doted upon. Or it could be that paranoia is genetic.

For once I was so pooped that I felt pretty good about trusting someone else with the kids. My sister, meantime, decided to tail Shirley to the playground. Not a supersleuth by any stretch of the imagination, Aunt Kooky was so nervous about being caught that she kept leaping behind cars and into shops until she got confused and lost track of Shirley and my kids after only a few blocks. Meanwhile, she could have been at my house helping me recover by making me a sandwich. Things are really more relaxing for me when I watch my own kids.

I'm not saying that I'm the best mother in the world. In fact there are probably people who could do a better job than I do with my kids. Like the day I got the old fish eye from all the professional nannies in the playground. They were having a kind of a coffee klatch while watching their kids, and I'm with my kids thinking, "Well, I'm actually actively engaged in playing with my own children, so I'm so great."

My daughter was playing in the sprinkler and took time out for a snack. I gave her a glass bottle of cran-raspberry juice and told her to be careful. She decided not to sit on a bench but to balance precariously in her wet bathing suit on a metal railing that divided the playground from the dirty, rocky, twig-laden hill that ran down the outside. So I'm thinking to myself, "That doesn't look so good," and all of a sudden she flipped over and was gone.

She went backward and rolled away down the hill. Luckily the bottle fell forward and smashed on the pavement of the playground. That shattering glass put everyone's attention on the crazy mom who lets her four-year-old drink from glass bottles and sit on narrow, slippery fences.

I went over the rail and pulled her up. She'd bruised and scratched her back and had a big bump on her head. I carried her over the broken bottle, trying to warn the other kids in the park away from all the bits of glass. The nannies were clearly disappointed. I'd done about twenty things wrong and all simultaneously. They all stared at me and rolled their professional nanny eyes.

Well, I'm not getting paid for this, I felt like saying to them. I'm not a professional—I'm just a mother. I didn't study for this. I have no license, no accreditation, no references. So fire me.

Thankfully, I've gotten over the nannies' reproach and I know how it all works now.

We'll gladly hire the nearest thirteen-year-old without an arrest record and hit the road. "I've got my cell phone!" I yell, as I peel out of the driveway. "Remember 9-1-1 will send an ambulance. Snacks in the fridge!"

36

---

aggravated devotion

One Saturday, three hours after the kids and I had gotten up, my husband emerged from the bedroom. That part was okay—it was the weekend, and we were letting Daddy sleep late, trying to keep it down. And though I'd awakened to a bowl that had contained tuna fish the night before, emptied but not rinsed, left on the counter all night long to get really smelly—in spite of that, I whipped up some coffee for my husband's eventual appearance. He's not good without coffee.

So around tenish, he stumbles into the living room and gently suggests, "Make me some toast." By this point I'd already taken multiple requests for toast and cereal and juice and milk and bananas from my kids, finally gotten to eat my own breakfast, and was sitting down to read a huge folder of work. I simply said, "If you want it now, you'd better pop it in yourself." The affront! The look of betrayal on his face. I tried to jolly him along. "Go ahead. I'll fix it for you when it pops, just put it in."

This episode ticked us both off for the rest of the day. Me because the extra three hours and the waiting coffee counted for nothing. Him because such a minor morning request was denied. To say he's not a morning person is a little like saying King Kong was a large monkey.

When we first met, my husband and I had a lot of fun: late nights, long walks, diner food, old movies. Ah, it was a heady time. He'd occasionally even pen me a little poem—well, maybe more of a limerick. Always silly but romantic nonetheless.

When we were still dating, we once had a big argument in Penn Station over his not rushing fast enough to make the train that I'd timed perfectly for us to get to by the skin of our teeth. If only he'd run a little faster!

To defuse the situation, he went over to one of those tourist souvenir stands and bought me a little pink stuffed mouse with suction cups on its paws. I don't know what pink mice have to do with New York tourism, but I thought it was a cute gesture. We named it Ignatz, and became a bit overly attached to it as a sign of our devotion to each other. As the years went by and we racked up more time as a married couple, we had fewer Ignatz moments and more toast moments.

Maybe it was the crazy pace of modern life with careers,

kids, and mortgages that distracted us from those romantic inclinations. But sometimes I wonder if men can ever really be like they are in movies, on television, and on the bookstore shelves—I mean, after ten years of marriage.

Especially in the olden days, men sent gifts, smothered women with attention, wrote love letters. Some of these guys could write really great love letters. There are books full of them. It makes me go all mushy just reading about how crazy these men were about their women. I couldn't even put together a pamphlet.

Of course, letter writing as communication is practically part of another era, one of different sensibilities. Everyone used to write letters way back when. When people were apart, there were no cell phones or E-mail or Palm Pilots. So when one found oneself in a different time zone late at night with less than 107 cable channels to flip through, one might sit down and write a letter to the object of one's affections and tell her how he felt about her—over and over again.

My husband and I weren't apart very much, so there was very little opportunity for us to write letters to each other. We communicated like crazy, chatting over breakfast and dinner, talking on the phone in between. We discussed things in the car. We sat on the porch and chewed the fat. We conferred during pitching changes of baseball games—mostly about how the bull pen wasn't going to have a chance if the Mets didn't start hitting the ball.

We were nearly always together, so the most information we ever committed to paper might be the occasional little note, such as, from him: "If you get a chance, and can tear yourself away from doing your nails and watching *The Young and the Restless,* call the exterminator about that beehive!"

Or from me: "The baby gets cereal with carrots for dinner. Not actual raw carrots—the baby kind in the jar. Don't forget to feed him!"

Even our home videos—the technology that gave us the excuse, "We don't have to write it down, we've got it all on tape"—couldn't capture the love. They usually showed my face up close telling my husband to stop filming me from two inches away and to save the batteries for when I brought out the cake. They often ended with me saying, "You're ruining everything."

But then one evening my husband got off the commuter train with a big bunch of flowers and handed them to me. If I looked surprised (and I did), it was because flowers in this marriage are usually reserved for anniversaries or as a follow-up to a big stinky fight. We'd had neither occur in our house for at least a couple of weeks.

"That's for being my girlfriend," he said.

This statement prompted a chorus of quips from the occupants of our three car seats. "Mommy's not your girlfriend!" our four-year-old son pointed out. "She's Mommy."

"Daddy!" giggled his six-year-old sister. The baby just gave a Bronx cheer.

It was pretty romantic, even though it wasn't a love letter or even a toy mouse.

37

school socks

A panic set in at my house. Logistics, scheduling, traffic patterns. You'd think we were planning the Millennium Summit. We were just getting ready for first grade.

The summer was gone, September had arrived, and that meant two things: the Mets were fading in the East and the mad scramble was on to get ready for the first day of school. The bus came at 7:37 in the morning—an ungodly hour, even for Catholic school. The suddenly cool weather had all three of my children (not to mention me) snug in bed with absolutely no intention of getting up.

There were going to have to be some major sleep-schedule

modifications if we were going to fit in luxuries like eating breakfast and brushing teeth.

My daughter had to be fully outfitted for her new parochial school. We'd gone to the uniform fitting in the spring, and the fast-talking saleslady from the uniform company talked me into buying practically everything. Two jumpers so one's always ready to go, three blouses, the school cardigan embroidered with school name, sweatshirt, sweatpants, shorts and T-shirt for gym class. Of course we could buy shoes elsewhere, but the shoes offered by the uniform company had the best arch support, and they promised a hard-to-find narrow width. I'm not a total pushover though—I passed on the socks. After all, you can get socks anywhere, and this was only May (but I couldn't resist the matching plaid headband and ponytail scrunchy).

Hey, when school started, I knew I'd be completely organized.

The package from the uniform company arrived a couple of weeks later. The plaid jumpers fit fairly well, but they were too long. Well, hemming is easy. The gym uniform, however, was bizarrely large for a six-year-old. Or it was just right for a bizarrely large six-year-old. It was almost big enough for me. At any rate, it would have to be exchanged. The shoes were the wrong size, and the uniform company told me on the phone that I was apparently suffering from a mild case of delusional psychosis, because they didn't carry narrow width after all.

Exchanges were made. Shoes were purchased (rubber-soled, sensible oxfords—not those popular clunky-heeled sling backs guaranteed to twist an ankle during the first hour of school). I began to relax about the whole thing. Then, with one day to go, my eyes bleary from hemming jumpers, I spoke to another mom on the phone. "I guess we're finally all ready for Wednesday," I said.

"Do you have socks?" the other mom asked me. Socks? I told her I had white anklets I thought would look cute.

She gasped, "You have to have navy blue kneesocks."

It all came back to me—that day in May. I could have ordered the official archdiocesan-approved navy blue kneesocks from the uniform company and been completely sartorially prepared for all parochial contingencies, but no, I knew I'd be able to find them anywhere. And I was betting I could find them for less.

Here's what I learned: navy blue kneesocks are impossible to find, especially if you wait until the day before school begins. Malls are not particularly concerned with Catholic school fashions. Belly shirts and low-rise pants for six-year-old girls, no problem. But no kneesocks.

How did my mom do it? Every day growing up, my sister and I walked those two city blocks to school with my socks staying up and hers falling down. But we both had our navy blue kneesocks.

The entire next day I was on the phone with a *Yellow Pages* in my lap. "Do you carry navy blue kneesocks?" Most store clerks could detect the pathetic desperation in my voice and just laughed sadistically at me, as if to say, "You'll never find them the day before school! What have you been doing all summer when you should have been ordering your child the proper navy blue kneesocks—lying around eating bonbons? Now your kid will be the only one in school with inappropriate socks! Why, I have half a mind to report you to the Child Welfare Bureau!"

It took some doing, but I found them. My daughter was off to her first day of grade school with sensible, narrow-width shoes and navy blue kneesocks—blissfully unaware of what her mother goes through to make her life run smoothly. As it should be.

I poured a cup of coffee and toasted my mom for consistent grace under pressure.

38

---

going back to the gym

.

The spring women's magazines appeared on the stands, each touting their surefire shape-up routines that would have us all wearing thong bikinis in six weeks.

Speaking for myself, it's never been bikini season for me. Even as a youngster, I was always the full-coverage tank suit kind of girl. Still, as the warm weather approaches, one can't help but think about working on the ol' figure a bit after a winter spent hiding under big pullovers and in sweatpants.

I'd managed to do away with most of my postpartum pudginess since having my son the previous fall, but I never exercised. The experts are right about one thing—you can't get in shape on diet alone. Everything on my body just sat there unless I was moving, in which case it jiggled. When my daughter asked me why my belly was so "ploppy," I decided to get moving.

My original plan was to power walk my way to fitness through the hilly streets of my Westchester town, but something always distracted me and I ended up staying at home or hopping in the car instead. My exercise tapes kept getting pushed behind *Aladdin* and *Tubby the Tuba*. No one at my house was willing to give me forty minutes alone with Billy Blanks to do tae-bo anyway. I needed to go to a place where I'd be forced to exercise. So I joined a gym.

It wasn't the first time. I'd belonged to plenty of gyms in the city before, but I usually got bored or lazy. Or I'd sit on the recumbent bike with my feet up on the computer console that told me how many miles per hour I was traveling (0) and how many calories I'd burned (0) and watch *Regis* on the gym-provided TV screens until the closed captioning gave me a headache.

But this time would be different.

I picked a gym only two minutes from my house, so I'd have a better shot at getting there. I walked in and was pounced on by the usual overzealous membership guy. He told me that the annual membership fee was $299 but for me he'd make it $99, and then he lowered the monthly fees by about $20 and I said, "Gee, thanks."

He showed me around. The place was filled with suburban moms (like me) dropping their kids at the babysitting room and filling their Evian bottles with water fountain water, and the overly pumped-up musclemen (not like me) talking lats and wondering where to find street clothes to fit their bizarre proportions.

Any questions, membership guy wanted to know.

"Where do you get the towels, at the desk?" I asked.

"Yes. They're one dollar each."

I was stymied. "You charge for towels? That's ridiculous."

"I know," he shrugged, "But let's sit down and talk about the good stuff."

"I don't think so."

He was pulling on my elbow, trying to yank me into his office. "A lot of members just bring a towel from home."

"But then I have to wash it. I can use three of your towels and stand on them and dry my feet and then put them in your hamper. That's the fun of coming to the gym. I don't think I'm joining."

"Over towels? You city people always expect free towels." (I swear he actually said this like we live in *Green Acres* or something.) "We don't have the same laundry facilities here."

I stared at him. "Okay," he sighed, "you can have free towels."

"Well, I don't want any special treatment. . . ."

"No, no, it's okay." And he wrote on the back of my membership card, "This person gets free towels."

I took my free towel and went straight to an aerobics class. I wanted to try one of those new trendy things like spinning or kick boxing, but there was only one class going on.

It was called Power Low, but it was a basic 1980s leg

warmers and headbands, Olivia Newton-John aerobics class. And not having taken one since the eighties, I almost collapsed. Just moving around for an hour was tough enough, but not knowing any of the steps made me feel like Lucy Ricardo sneaking into one of Ricky's dance numbers at the Tropicana without bothering to learn the routine. I was crashing into people and looking like a klutz, not just feeling like one. I could see myself in the mirror, and I looked stupid.

But it made me sweat and the next day I was in a lot of pain, so I was optimistic about getting into condition. I'd be buff, I'd be lean, I'd be camera ready. Well, maybe not, but at least the towels were free.

39

movie star hair

The only time I'd ever gone to the beauty parlor was when I needed a change. It happened about twice a year. After all, I'd worn my hair the same way for practically my whole life.

When I was a kid, I had a pageboy cut, kind of a Prince Valiant look. My cousin Kelly, who was a little older, wore her straight blond hair long and parted in the middle. It was the early 1970s, and I thought she was the coolest, most beautiful girl in the world. One day, after visiting with her, I went home and stuck bobby pins in my bangs to make them stay over at the sides. I decided I would part my hair in the middle and grow it long like Kelly's. And I did. Ever since, I'd worn my hair in some version of that long style. For a change, in the eighties I started parting it on the side.

Lately change was not a product of boredom but of necessity. My very straight hair that had always fallen smoothly was starting to pouf out unless I blew it dry. Grays were popping up in front and sticking straight up. I plucked despite my mother's warning that if I plucked one I would get ten more. Was she right, or was I just old?

At first I thought that since I needed a fresh look, short was the way to go. Sharon Stone and Annette Bening had nice short cuts. But they're famous movie stars, and I was picturing them at the Oscars. I bet they didn't just wash and go. When the paparazzi caught up with them on regular days and splashed their photos all over the supermarket tabloids, the actresses always seemed to be wearing baseball caps. Was that so they wouldn't be recognized or because they were having bad hair days?

I'd gone with a short look a few years earlier, but my daughter got very upset. When I picked her up from preschool, she burst into tears.

"You don't look like my mommy, you look like Lucia." (Lucia's a friend of mine who's an actual real person with the cutest short haircut. But she has wavy hair and a fabulous face.) My daughter told me to go to the machine that puts your hair back on.

My husband, who usually accused me of chickening out of a short look, seemed pleased. He blurted something about it being like having a new wife. He immediately became confused and tried to backpedal when his helpful remark was met with a scowl.

In spite of his oafish remark, I liked having short hair. Except that when I woke up, it stuck straight up in the air. Once it settled, though, it could feel pretty cool. But some days I looked like Dorothy Hamill, which was a good thing back in the seventies. Those were the days I pulled out the old baseball cap, just like Annette and Sharon.

So I tried to be realistic and started looking at women in the supermarket. Perhaps I'd find a woman with a great cut and could ask her who did her hair. Well, it wasn't the same as flipping through *Vogue*. I saw a lot of scrunchie-tied hair, butterfly-cinched twists, baseball caps, bandannas, roots, gray hair—it was the real world.

On the weekend, when my husband could watch the kids, I couldn't get an appointment at the "good" salon in town, so I decided to try the other beauty parlor. I still didn't know what I wanted. They gave me a bunch of hairstyle books, and the only thing I could find that I liked was a "before" picture. The woman in the photo looked cute before—but after she looked kind of like Sylvester Stallone's second wife.

I haltingly asked the hairdresser if she remembered Demi Moore's hair in *Ghost*. (Another movie star!) "But that would mean heavy bangs," she said. "Is that what you want?" Not really. I was clueless and nervous about making a big hair mistake.

"What you need, hon, is some color."

The thought terrified me. I'd made it almost forty years

without ever coloring my hair. I'd had nice light brown hair for many years, but once I started working and missed summers in the sun, my hair turned very dark brown. But for many years it was still shiny and nice.

Lately, my hair seemed like a brown hat. Maybe women my age did need a pick-me-up, but I was pretty nervous. "Don't worry," said the stylist. "I'll do lowlights that will just be another shade of brown and will give your hair depth. People won't even know that you colored your hair, but it will brighten up and look healthier."

The other stylists smiled and nodded. I was outnumbered. Could I argue with this woman who was about to charge me an arm and a leg?

No, she was a professional and probably right. And I only spent about two dollars a month on my hair by purchasing a large bottle of shampoo and conditioner in one—on sale. If I put together all the times I hadn't spent money on my hair, I deserved this pampering.

She brought out charts and graphs and explained how she was going to formulate a very special color to go with my hair, and she would only apply it to key strands and time it perfectly to come out just right.

It sounded good to me, so I put myself in her capable hands.

Then she dumped a quart of straight bleach and peroxide on my hair and went into the back room to eat two slices of pizza.

When I was rinsed and the towel came off, I saw some extremely light-looking lines running through my very dark hair. I began to pray. I figured maybe it was the light in the salon. Maybe it would look better when it was dry. I waited as she dried and brushed it out. I had a weird smile plastered on my face as I watched in the mirror.

"Are you okay, hon? Don't you like it?"

"No, no, it's great. Yeah, it's really subtle." What the hell was wrong with me?

I looked around the salon at the stylists and their own unique hair colorings. How could I have entrusted my virgin head to this group?

I gave them all my money, tipped them heavily, and ran for my life. I came out into the sunlight looking like a cheap skunk.

My family greeted me with the same fake smiles plastered on their faces. My daughter had learned diplomacy since kindergarten. "Is that what you wanted, Mommy?"

"No, honey, really," said my husband, in an overly sincere way, "it looks great."

"No, they're not that blond."

Lulu was appalled when she came to visit. "At least you don't see people up here," she said.

I found a box of temporary brown hair color at the supermarket for seven dollars and washed it into my hair. It toned down the stripes and I continued to use it until the streaks finally began to grow out.

Some friends said I should have gone back to the village salon and made them fix it free of charge. But I was afraid of what might happen. And would they call me a liar for saying I liked it? I lived in fear with my blond streaks, crossing the street whenever I walked past the shop.

40

---

all out of feng shui

My hair was a disaster and now my energy was being blocked by karmic clutter. My house had no feng shui. Nothing followed that ancient design philosophy of balance and harmony that should exist in one's surroundings to benefit the dweller.

I read a book of feng shui guidelines, how to have lots of positive energy in one's home, and unfortunately all of our harmony was flying out the windows, the heart of the house was covered with cooking grease and take wood, and we had too many doors. If anything, our house was anti–feng shui. We couldn't even pronounce feng shui.

The way I'd arranged my furniture (the wrong way) was

distracting me from the important things in my life. And that messy garden shed in the far left corner of our yard was actually preventing financial success.

We'd had an attic room lined with empty crawl spaces and a large unfinished portion of our basement behind the family room. After only a short time in the house, these areas were filled with boxed files, bags of outgrown baby clothes, memorabilia from high school—all the junk I had to stick somewhere when the California Closet lady came over—as well as stuff I'd offered to store for friends who still lived in the city and had no storage space (I wanted to show off how much room we had now that we'd made the jump to the suburbs).

I thought if you had storage space it was to be used for storage. Apparently not. According to the feng shui experts, clutter not only collects dust, it ruins lives. And it wasn't just the clutter, it was the bad mojo it gave off, causing husbands to say dumb things without any reasonable forethought. Asking your wife all the time, "When are we going to start getting some feng shui going around here?" is bad feng shui.

I think that thinking about feng shui, planning for it, should count. Feng shui doesn't come cheap. You need financing for quality feng shui. Oh, they say you don't need to spend, just rearrange and clear and tie some bells on. But my front door was in the wrong place, and all our good fortune was making a hasty retreat through the living room window. It also seemed to be affecting our digestions, making us fat, lazy, and depressed.

If you look at the feng shui happy house map, our kitchen

would be the heart of our house. It was a mess. It needed a complete overhaul. It's not just a question of taste; it was nobody's taste. The cabinet doors were falling off and the drawers didn't open, and the dishwasher was a good four steps away from the sink. Two of the four burners on top of the stove didn't work, the rubber trim that kept the refrigerator closed was falling off and was held in place with Scotch tape, and there was no counter space. Not like, "Oh, couldn't we all use a little more counter space"—there was literally *no* counter space. I had to put plates on top of the coffee machine or the microwave as I dished out food from the stove.

The floor was an ugly old tile that never looked clean, and there had been a tiny counter near the door that a previous owner had probably put there just to have a counter, but it stuck out and was not really useful. When my three-year-old crashed into its very pointy corner with his head, my husband pulled it out, which took no effort at all. Except for the fact that underneath was bright orange tile that had not been replaced with the newer dirty-look tile, so now we had a large orange rectangle in the middle of our kitchen floor with nothing to show for it.

It was an ugly kitchen, and I knew it because even the most polite guests stopped short when they saw it and asked about our plans to renovate it. It was an eyesore. When I had the family room rug replaced after the sewer incident, the carpet guys said as they passed through the kitchen, "You know, we could give you a new floor in here." People asked if we couldn't take out a home equity loan if it was money holding us back from a new kitchen. It was bumming everyone's feng shui high.

Bad feng shui isn't only clutter but unfinished projects. Well, we hadn't even started on the kitchen, and I was sure the Scotch tape on the fridge was very constricting to our vitality levels. But a house that's too neat is energetically sterile, said one expert. That was good for us because our house was not overly tidy. That gave me inner peace.

a week in the life

I began keeping a diary, thinking I could turn it into a book. After all, I used to fill journals all the time when I was younger. Who am I? What is life? What is my destiny?

And now, as the chronicle of a woman raising three children, trying to keep it all together, it could be pretty compelling stuff. It would be like *The Nanny Diaries* without the help, style, or money.

Forget it. I only kept the thing going for a week. I'd need a nanny to be able to keep a proper diary.

Here's what I managed.

KEY:

N: *two-year-old toddler*

J: *four-year-old boy*

S: *six-year-old girl*

Snowball: *family cat*

D: *nondriving, forty-year-old husband*

Diarist: *extremely tired forty-year-old mother*

MONDAY: Resolve to eat more bran and exercise daily.

Meet 7:37 school bus by skin of our teeth, lunchbox and backpack akimbo, me in flannel pajamas. **S.** safely gone until 2:45. **J., N.,** and & I shuffle back to drink coffee (me) and eat waffles square by square (them).

Drop husband at 8:23 train and drop off **J.** at pre-K. Everyone's car looks cleaner than mine. It's purple day and **J.,** wearing a purple T-shirt, insists that Barney is not a dinosaur but a happy bear.

Kisses, hugs, love you's, and partial freedom for two hours and thirty-five minutes. Violate 10 mph limit leaving the school grounds since no kids are in sight.

Hit the highway at 60 mph to make the low-impact class at the gym in four minutes.

Put little guy in babysitting room. Watch doorknob turn frantically and pathetic cries of "Momma! Momma!"

Walk into class late and get look you get when you only show up once a month. Confuse grapevine and pony—biggest klutz in the class. Also wore wrong bra, elastic shot, serious support issues. Upset older man in back row.

Too rushed to shower. Collect traumatized toddler and hit supermarket and CVS before pre-K dismissal.

Chess club and Brownies.

Homework, playground, burgers, and bed.

Forgot to eat bran.

TUESDAY: **N.** has pink eye. Darn germy babysitting room. Went for drops. $33 copay. Stopped in bagel shop to cheer him up. Grabbed a bran muffin.

Vacuum minivan but not house. Found $1.78 and four cups of Cheerios. Seven mummified McD's fries.

Take **N.** to deserted playground so he can play without stigma of contagion.

(Kristen's birthday party–buy gifts.)

Nuke chicken nuggets.

Snowball peed in family room again.

WEDNESDAY: Saw Sue Ellen at CVS. She'd bought three shirts at Marshall's for thirty dollars. What a shopper. Baby better.

Stopped at dry cleaners, post office, Shop Rite. Bought five packs of spaghetti for two dollars today–essential and good budgeting. **D.** brought home posthumous Joey Ramone CD– nonessential and bad budgeting.

N. took a nap! Bonus hour. Wrote. Avoided vacuuming.

Snowball to vet. No physical problems. Cat anxious. Me, too. Vet suggests Prozac. For cat, not me.

Spaghetti for everyone

THURSDAY: **S.** and **J.** both have pink eye. Coerced pediatrician into giving me sample drops to avoid bankruptcy. Everyone stays home.

N. learns how to say, "I keek yo butt! I keek yo butt!" Then he kicks the air and falls down. Snowball stops peeing in the family room and starts peeing at the base of curtains. Used another gallon of Pee-Away and spoke sternly to cat.

Finally got out of the house about eight o'clock and took a walk to the video store. Two teenagers are hanging out in front—a boy wearing a Bobby Sherman puka shell necklace, smoking a Parliament, and a girl who works in the store with him. He is telling her about a parking lot run-in with a village police officer:

> And I'm like, "dude." And he's like, "Step this way." And I'm like, "Huh"? And he's like pushing me with his clipboard. I shoulda taken him down, seriously, dude. He was whacked.

She nods sympathetically.

No one seems to be running the video store. I fantasize that maybe we'll move back to the city before the kids are teenagers.

FRIDAY: Kids addicted to Joey Ramone's version of "What a Wonderful World." The boys jump around in a really punk way. Cute now—will hate it when they're sixteen and want to hang at CBGBs (dude!).

Pick up **D.** at 5:42. Kids' eyes better. Meet Sue Ellen and brood for pizza 6:00–7:15. She wears another cute Marshall's outfit. I rethink my sweatshirt-and-cargo-pants look. Free music show at the elementary school. Nice but no Ramones. Everyone exhausted and cranky.

SATURDAY: Twelve to 2:00, Tori's birthday party. Buy gift. Two to 4:00, Eddie's birthday party. Buy gift. Stay and chaperone at bowling alley because four-year-olds bowl overhand.

Snowball pees on clean laundry. Becomes an outdoor cat.

Family Fun Night 5:00–7:00 p.m. Hot dogs in the church hall; kids run themselves ragged.

Nine p.m.: Date night. Watch the *E! True Hollywood Story* of *The Love Boat* cast and eat candy from Eddie's and Tori's goody bags.

SUNDAY: Ten a.m.: Late and rumpled for church in sweatshirt and cargo pants. Parked in no-parking zone. Priest watches our large group enter in the middle of his homily. **N.** ran up center aisle doing the "I keek your butt" routine. Swore at him and threatened to beat him. I did, not the priest. Think I broke three commandments just during mass.

Home for quiet family Sunday. **D.** mulches yard. I read papers. Kids play Monopoly for an hour without a fight. Snowball stretches happily in sunny backyard. And I say to myself, "What a wonderful world . . ."

42

---

is this chapter
tax deductible?

I made a fortune at the market. No, not Wall Street—Shop
Rite. I bought two boxes of special millennium cheddar
cheese Goldfish crackers, which means the little fish have
funny party hats on and are not getting any fresher. They
were two for four dollars but they rang up as two forty-nine
each. When I got home, I saw the overcharge on my receipt.
My husband thought it wasn't worth it to claim the dollar (really ninety-eight cents) they owed me, but I go there all the
time anyway and a dollar's a dollar. Except this time, a dollar
was three forty-seven. They told me at the service desk that
their error meant a refund of the overcharged difference plus
the cost of one full-price item. I studied the numbers, saw

where I could make a dollar, and made three and a half times that. I'm still trying to make up for all that expensive aluminum foil I bought at the all-night deli in the city.

This was the high point of my yearly financial investment success.

A lot of friends were complaining about the stock market—how they'd lost so much in recent months. What a killer the economy was on the old nest egg. Suddenly I felt lucky about never having a dime to invest. We hadn't lost anything at all by investing. Our nest egg wasn't withering away because ours had never been laid. We had a nest, but no eggs. All our money's safely invested in credit-card debt.

We'd opened up an account intended to be a savings plan for our kids' education. It was supposed to be for college, but it ended up getting spent on preschool. Preschool is really expensive. And anyway, our kids were smart. They would probably qualify for scholarships if they kept up their studies. Especially the baby. I started playing those Mozart make-your-baby-smarter tapes just in case.

We'd had a little money once before the kids were born, and my husband and I had got the idea into our heads that we should get into the stock market. We conducted some research (we must have read, or at least skimmed, three or four business magazines) and decided to invest in some individual stocks that were described as promising. Now, we weren't going to gamble in some fly-by-night Internet stuff. No, we would buy steel. I mean, what's more solid than steel?

Every day we looked up the abbreviations on the stocks

pages and saw the stocks just sit there. Then they started to fall. Our five-hundred-dollar investment was shrinking. Stories began to appear about the poor performance of our particular companies. The headlines might as well have read, "Konigs buy steel; industry collapses!" Finally we bailed out, cursing the companies.

I recently looked them up. The first one I couldn't find; they're probably on the lam. The other one is at seven. We bought it at around thirty and got out at nineteen. So buying the stock was a bad idea, but getting out was a good idea.

At least we had three little deductions. Kids were good for that every April 15. Four, if you counted the house we bought to put our three little deductions into. Everyone could appreciate the wonders of those three little words: mortgage interest deductible.

But I wanted more deductions. Yes, I was one of those horrible, selfish, mean-spirited people who think that shelling out 40 percent of our hard-earned dough in taxes was a bit excessive. I felt terrible about it—all that money going to pay for good, efficient government services. But my husband and I just couldn't shake that greedy impulse to foolishly spend our own money on frivolous things like groceries and clothes and school for our kids.

I wanted more deductions, and I didn't want to have to go through four months of morning sickness, another C-section, and inevitable jelly belly to get them. If only I'd put my kids in daycare last year instead of looking after them myself, I could get that child-care credit. But since I stayed home with them and worked around their needs and schedules, I got bupkus.

I'd misplaced my priorities as far as the IRS was concerned. Motherhood took up most of my time, all of it actually. Even when I was working, the kids were interrupting me. When I was sleeping, the kids were waking me up. When I was in the bathtub . . . well, you get the picture.

Doesn't wash with Uncle Sam. But if I'd spent less time with my kids, I'd have been rewarded. Still, it was partially my fault—I could have earned more deductions if I'd been a little savvier in my business dealings.

If I'd gone out for more three-martini lunches (well, any martini lunches), I could deduct those. I should have sent expensive gifts to people I work with. Or I might have flown off on business trips like that mom in the commercial who tells her kid she'll buy him a bike for his birthday because she has to be away, and in the end, she takes him on the trip with her. She probably wrote off the bike, too, as a necessary business supply. Meanwhile I stayed home and made jelly sandwiches and rented Blockbuster movies and none of that was deductible. And I paid for my own bikes.

My failures in the deduction game go on and on:

- Because I didn't spend a year in Provence, I had no foreign housing expenses.
- I didn't use any gasoline for farming purposes—unless fueling up the lawnmower counts.
- I couldn't deduct my uniform of denim shirt and

overalls as protective clothing even though it protected me from spit-up and drool.

- I might possibly list as a bad debt the Time-Life home-improvement books that my husband ordered in a burst of completely out-of-character, late-night do-it-yourself enthusiasm (that quickly waned) and then forgot to cancel so they just kept coming. We used them to prop up a broken bed slat. Or maybe that was a major capital improvement.

- Luckily there were those never-ending educational loans from my two stints in grad school. All that lingering interest was deductible.

If only I'd married a millionaire like they do on TV. Instead, I married a thousandaire.

Lulu was still looking for a millionaire but having no luck. Oh, she found a couple but they were not the right millionaires. One guy had about forty million good reasons to go out with him. Unfortunately, if she'd married him, she'd have spent all his money on therapy. To quote Lulu, "I would rather live in a shack than have to live with that loser and all his money in his Upper East Side townhouse."

And if that multimillionaire is so vain that he thinks this anecdote is about him, well, Lulu's been out with plenty of multimillionaires so unless you're "the loser," we're not talking about you. Still, she was hoping to find someone good. He could even be short if his wallet was fat enough to stand on.

Me, I went on a blind date with a perfectly nice guy in a

secondhand sports coat who bought me toast and chamomile tea because I was deathly ill with bronchitis. I would have canceled the date but I didn't have his number. I had to show up or be totally rude. Somehow, in my ill condition, he thought enough of me to ask me out again. I was too sick to meet him, and he showed up at my apartment with an Etch-a-Sketch to make me feel better. Our second real date was over coffee and pie at the Astor Place Coffee Shop and an escorted subway ride home to Brooklyn, as neither of us had the cab fare. I quit smoking (more savings!) and married him.

So now, no matter what, we have each other—and our three little tax deductions.

43

---

financially challenged

Life was good. We were happy. We were settled. We were broke.

We'd spent nine years making sure I could be home full time with the kids. It was good for them and for me. But I wasn't really making any money. My husband was—but we were a one-income family with two-income expenses.

The "gentle reminders" from various companies to whom we were in debt turned to irritating "warnings," then to pesky "final turn-off" notices, and finally to those headache-inducing "intent to foreclose" and "imminent lien" letters.

Luckily, the benevolent and charitable credit-card offers

came in with incredibly low rates for a limited time, and we began juggling our debt from one account to the next, jumping before rates went up and spreading things out. Unfortunately, we began to skip a couple of payments here and there. The credit-card companies were very understanding—they quadrupled our rates overnight.

Our lazy evenings spent watching rented movies and eating low-fat frozen yogurt turned into stressful nights spent discussing the seemingly insurmountable money problems that were piling up by the day.

We were even late on our mortgage payments, the ultimate sin, we would find out.

Looking for work seemed harder than ever; money fears keeping us slightly weak in the knees. I realized why people bought lottery tickets. There are times when it seems that a big problem can only be fixed by a great big solution. But, with luck, and a few good hours of sleep, we woke up one day understanding that little steps could lead us to the place where we wanted to be.

Finally, we were encouraged by a friend to try credit counseling. We discovered there are two kinds: for-profit and not-for-profit.

The for-profit are a slick group who will take all kinds of risks on your behalf—sort of. Here was the scenario. We were to ignore the credit-card company threats and sheriff's notices for about three months. By that time our creditors would be so happy to get anything out of us that they would be sure to settle for about a third of what we owed. Either that or we'd be in jail. We asked the debt-consolidation company if this approach would ruin our credit.

Could it get any worse? they answered.

What about the twenty phone calls a day?

Don't pick up.

They wanted a few hundred dollars from us up front for the privilege of sharing this great idea for handling credit problems.

We decided to see what the not-for-profit folks had to say for themselves.

This group contacted the credit-card companies immediately and told them that they were handling things now and not to call us anymore. The phone went blessedly silent. We sent the credit-counseling company a certain amount every month once we'd realistically looked at the money that was coming in and our actual expenses for keeping food in the kitchen, a car in the driveway, and a roof over our heads. They also helped us by suggesting we take a close look at calling plans, Internet services, and other monthly bills. Turns out we were being overcharged all over the place. I changed a few plans, canceled some stuff, and ended up saving hundreds a year.

After a couple of months, seeing that we were on time and sincere, most of the companies dropped the usurious interest rates down to something decent, and the late fees stopped being added on. All except for one company that would not lower the rate, and we hate them.

Our credit-card situation was finally coming under control, and we were about to see what life was like without those little evil pieces of plastic. That's right, as part of the agreement, all accounts were closed and we were on our own, about to learn if we could survive on the money we made.

44

---

house for sale

The answer was no. We could not survive on the money we were making. The credit counseling gave us some hope for the future, and we began to be more aggressive about looking for work, but things were slow and we still had a mortgage, a car, and a family to pay for. We're talking without perks: just food, clothes, doctors.

The gym, the cleaning ladies, the Blockbuster rentals, and the fancy bad haircuts went away. I started walking the hills for exercise. Not only free but effective. Lots of fresh air, and I could keep tabs on what the neighbors were up to.

We cleaned the house ourselves, though not to my husband's satisfaction. But we tried.

We discovered free videos and DVDs at the public library. They even had some classics the rental stores didn't.

I was still in recovery from my last trip to the beauty parlor, so that wasn't such a loss. I was only on the third step: loathing. I'd gotten through horror and shame pretty well. Life was spent in a ponytail these days anyway.

The late-night discussions about money continued, and it suddenly dawned on us that all was not lost. Though we tended to think of ourselves as people with no investments—nothing in the stock market, no CDs, no money market funds, no art, we didn't even own our car, we leased it—we were sitting on a major investment.

Our house.

Yes, in just a couple of years, our little bungalow had appreciated a lot. About 40 percent more than we'd paid for it. We suddenly realized that if we could sell the house and buy a cheaper house, we could settle our debts and lower our monthly expenses significantly. We could have an emergency fund in the bank in case we had another dry spell like the one we'd just gone through. Our very own nest egg.

But where were the cheap houses? Go north, youngish family!

It was true. If we left our tony county of Westchester outside of New York City and went up the Hudson River a couple of counties, we might get a bigger house, with more land for less money, adding only about a half hour or so on the train each way to the city for my husband. Hey, he liked to read and look out the window. It was a sacrifice we were willing to make.

We asked my sister to watch the kids while we drove north. After about thirty-five minutes or so, we found a proliferation of houses in our price range, some with up to an acre of land! It looked like we would be able to make the switch. The ranches we saw were all roomy and in good condition, but I hoped something really special would pop up.

Then we found it, a gorgeous Victorian in perfect condition in a little village easily traveled on foot that had a wonderful school for our kids and was a three-minute drive to the train.

The Realtor called it a jewel and said the doorframes alone were worth a fortune because of the lovely wood. I think it was oak.

It was perfect.

Okay—it had a snake. A big snake. A python. Burmese.

It seems the owner had moved, but had left his snake behind. He came to feed it every couple of days, we were told.

All I know is that when we saw the house, I was drooling over the brand-new country kitchen, the great wooden staircase, the clawfoot bathtub, and the stained-glass details. As I walked into the fourth bedroom, I froze. On the floor was a giant glass tank that was inhabited by an eight-foot snake.

The empty room and the glass sides of the tank sort of gave you the feeling that this creature was not quite contained. I'd never seen anything like it outside of a zoo.

Later my neighbor asked me, "Does the house have that snake smell?"

Now that she mentioned it, the house did smell kind of like old socks, but that new kitchen was great, and I was sure the smell would go away when the snake went. I just hoped that there had always been just one snake and that there was no slithery friend lurking in the walls waiting to come out for a snack after the closing. I was sure this wouldn't sour the deal or keep me up at night once we closed. After all, that kitchen!

I came back to inspect the house with an engineer a few days later. While I was standing outside looking at the garden, an unassuming man parked across the street and walked toward me with a cardboard box tucked under his arm. We smiled at each other.

"Are you the prospective buyer?" he asked.

"Are you the owner?"

I told him how nice I thought the house was, and he told me that if I needed any information on caring for the plants and flowers in the yard he'd be glad to leave instructions.

"But don't leave the snake, har har," I said.

"I'm going to feed him now." He gestured to the box.

"What's in there?"

"Rats."

"Oh."

"Are they alive?"

"Not for long."

"Oh."

"I'll bop them on the head before I feed him, so he doesn't get bitten."

A regular little bunny foufou this guy was.

But I was undaunted. The engineering went well and this fellow would take his snake and I'd get that nice deep bathtub.

We were ready to jump. We put our house on the market, hiding the sign around the side of the house when the school bus pulled up that afternoon. We sat the kids down and explained the whole thing.

They had questions. They wanted to know about school. Could they stay with their friends? We had planned to pull them out at Christmastime, but I told them that maybe I would drive them back the half hour to school every day for six months so they could finish the year with their friends. I wasn't thinking about snowstorms and traffic and how I have trouble getting them out in front of my house in my pajamas to catch the school bus every morning, and now I was going to somehow have all three ready about an hour earlier to leave for the whole day and what was I going to do, sit in my car for six and a half hours? Volunteer more at the school. That was something I wanted to do, but that would absolutely end my already suffering work life. I was clearly losing it.

It was almost Halloween. "Will be still be able to trick-or-treat on our street with our friends?" That much we could promise.

All manner of real estate agents and prospective home

buyers began to tromp through our house. Usually I loitered outside so they could look freely. I heard all sorts of opinions about our house:

"Something has to be done about this kitchen. I mean, it's barely functional."

"Is this porch crooked or is it me? Is that a structural problem?"

"Oh, look how cute—crayon on the walls."

"The bathroom's got some mildew."

We were constantly battling to keep it clean and, still, someone found mildew. I felt like yelling, "People do live here, you know! You try to keep it clean with three kids and a cat!"

Still, mildew, crayon, and all, within a week we got a full-price offer on our house, and it looked like this thing was going to work.

45

---

free housebreaking wee-wee pad
with every purchase

When the chips are down and life is in turmoil and you're not sure what your next move should be and you have a lot of trouble keeping your household organized, what is the most logical step to take?

Get a dog, of course.

Not just any dog. A big dumb dog that will jump on you and chew up everything in the house and turn everything upside down and curtail your social life because you have to get home and walk the dog.

"Wait a minute, don't come in yet, the dog will jump."

"Sorry, the dog is excited."

"Sorry, the dog is barking."

"Sorry, we're idiots and we got a dog."

Intellectually, we knew all this stuff and we went ahead and got a dog anyway. We had a cat so, of course, we needed a dog, and a dog would fit in better while the cat was still young, and we had room and three kids need a dog and it would be fun.

We never could have gotten a dog in the city. Besides the dilemma of having to wait for an elevator, go down ten flights, and then get through a large lobby before making it to the curb, we had had a neighbor who hated dogs.

If someone left a dog home alone in their apartment for the day and the dog started barking, this guy who reminded me of Raymond Burr in *Rear Window* because he mysteriously came and went at odd hours with valises—would lean out the window and yell in a booming voice, "Control your dog!" Not only would dogs calm down after that, city traffic seemed to quiet for a few seconds.

Safe in the dog-friendly suburbs, I wanted a toy poodle. A perfect little lap dog that would fit in a tote bag and be no trouble at all. No one else was too enthusiastic about this plan. My husband wanted a beagle, his favorite dog, and he also was not about to spend a thousand dollars that we didn't have on a purebred poodle.

The whole point is to rescue a dog, he said. Go to the pound and get one.

I started frequenting the local animal shelters, which were full of adult pit bulls and German shepherds barking their heads off. I really didn't want a big dog, and the kids wanted a puppy. Those were hard to find in a dog shelter. There were no poodles at all.

I found a cute little pit bull puppy who seemed very sweet, so I asked about it. They said I couldn't adopt it with small kids because this dog, no matter how mild-mannered, would grow up to have powerful jaws of certain death.

I found a young beagle, not a puppy but cute, and they said I couldn't adopt it because it was sure to run off the first time my kids left the door open. I was beginning to think that no one in the pet-adoption business ever wanted to let anyone adopt.

Finally I called a rescue group listed on the Internet, and a young man answered. He told me that his family ran a foster home for many homeless dogs, and that I was welcome to come to his house to look around.

"We have a black puppy," he told me. "She's cute. Probably ten or twelve weeks old. You can have her if you come get her. I think she's a lab/cocker spaniel mix. She'll probably get to medium size."

Then he told me his mother worked at the local pet supply store and that I could speak to her for more information. I had a talk with her that made me feel better about going to a stranger's house that might possibly be a white slavery ring or the headquarters of a cult.

On the phone the woman who worked at the pet store told me that her son knew everything about the dogs and their shots.

"If you want the dog, she's yours. There's a fee, and we'll

give you some food to get you started." She mentioned that the next morning her family was leaving on a vacation, and the puppy would be left in the house with six other dogs to be fed and walked by volunteer neighbors.

My husband came home early, so I asked my daughter if she wanted to go check out the dog. "She'll want it if you take her with you," my spouse warned. I knew he was right, but maybe it would be the ugliest puppy we ever saw and we'd be able to say no.

We took off to a neighboring cottage community that is built on hills with winding roads twisting dangerously up and down. It was snowy and icy, and there was barely room for two cars to pass each other.

As we wound up the icy hills, my daughter suggested we turn back, which says a lot about how bad the driving must have been if a little girl on her way to get a new puppy wants to turn back. She knew I had no idea where I was going.

Finally we found the address, and there were a bunch of little kids sloshing around in a snowy yard being watched by older kids, all chasing a funny little pudgy black puppy. We got out and found the boy in charge. I spoke with him while my daughter joined in, chasing the puppy and trying to pick up the wriggling ball of a dog.

She was a cute thing. Black with white on her chin and on the tips of three paws. I couldn't figure out what she was. But I couldn't imagine the poor pup being alone with seven other dogs in a house for twelve days.

The boy gave me her medical records, and I gave him a

check to keep the rescues going. I asked if there was a simple way to get out of there. Everyone laughed somewhat manically.

We hauled the little dog into the car, and she fell asleep in my daughter's lap. I looked in the rearview mirror, and my daughter smiled at me.

I managed to wind down the hills and make it back to civilization.

We arrived at home, and my husband and the boys came out to see. "That's not a beagle," said my husband.

But she was accepted and a leash purchased, and she was named Cookie because she looked like an Oreo.

That night she pooped about twenty-seven times all over the house, and I was running around with rubber gloves and cleanser and sprays, looking like an old drunk from lack of sleep. I never remembered being that tired with the kids. It was like having a baby with no diapers who could run.

I took Cookie to the vet and had her treated for intestinal parasites. They looked at her and said, "This is no lab/cocker mix. This is a newfie."

A newfie?

"A Newfoundland. This is a hundred-pound-plus dog."

A newfie. So much for my toy poodle.

"Oh, and she has mange."

46

---

environmentally challenged

One day, while walking our mangy (yet adorable) mutt, I met up with a friend in our town who was very active in environmental causes. We talked about the sign in front of our place and the new house farther up the river valley.

She said, "Don't move north without talking to me first. There are some serious issues in some areas of that county with water and contamination."

I'd heard about some communities east of where we wanted to live where certain industries, over time, had allowed pollutants to get into the ground water, and now it was turning up in people's wells and there was a big cleanup and filtration system project underway. But we would be miles from there in a village with its own municipal water system, and it wasn't a problem.

"Just let me send you some files," she suggested.

She e-mailed me a bunch of newspaper articles about the problems they'd been having up there, and there was nothing I hadn't heard about until I saw the name of our intended new town and the mention of a cross street at the bottom of our new road. The road our new house was on.

I clicked on the file and read about an old industrial site there that was classified as a "class 2 inactive hazardous waste site." There was the suggestion that there would be "some danger to public health" living there.

I was stunned. On the day we found the Victorian, I'd asked our Realtor about that site when she was showing us how to get to the train station.

"What's that?" I asked. It looked like an abandoned factory.

"Oh, that's an abandoned factory," she said. "It's been closed for years."

That much was true. It had shut down in 1990. But before that it had been an industrial site since the 1830s. First, it produced gas for gas lamps, then felt hats. Until the 1970s—when environmental protection became all the rage—all the factory owners had just dumped stuff into the soil, a lagoon on the property, and the adjacent creek that ran through the village.

I started learning acronyms for contaminants and what they did. They potentially did a lot of really bad things.

This is where you try to rationalize, to put a good face on

things. I tried to make light of the fact that it had also been a hat company. That couldn't have been bad.

"That's the worst!" my activist friend told me. "They used mercury to stiffen the hats. That's where the expression 'mad as a hatter' came from: mercury poisoning."

Indeed, there was mercury in the soil. What became of the mad hatters, I don't know. Who knew fedoras were so dangerous?

Anyway, it turns out this place didn't even have a fence around it, and kids were seen ice skating on the frozen, glowing lagoon in the winter.

If we lived in that darling house, maybe I'd just have to tell the kids, "Go out and play, but go right. Never go left."

I contacted someone from the Department of Environmental Conservation who offered to send me a report on the site. It included all the details along with a map that basically showed our new house, the factory site, and the kids' new school, all within spitting distance.

I called the DEC agent and asked him about the site report.

"Well, some sites are not so serious, but class two is hazardous."

"Are they going to clean it up?"

"The company is out of business and the government is out of money."

"Would you live there?" I asked him.

"Nope."

That was it. This wasn't something someone could just

pick up and take away like that eight-foot python in my new bedroom. We backed out right before contracts were signed. We explained why we'd decided against the deal. The Realtor pled ignorance. The owner said nothing. The python was suspiciously quiet.

Meanwhile, the potential buyer for our old house had been fighting with his wife over kitchens, and she won. There was a place on the market a few streets away from our house that had a brand-new kitchen and lots of feng shui. I can't blame her. That's what I was going for.

In fact the whole process was kind of feng shui-y because of the way it worked out. We didn't have a house to buy and our house didn't have a buyer.

And I think industrial waste is probably anti–feng shui. And snakes, too, at least in bedrooms.

So we took the sign down and pulled our house off the market and went back to the way it was before. Keeping it clean for prospective buyers was hell anyway.

47

these are the good old days

So we were back where we started.

Except we had almost a year's worth of credit counseling under our belts and our credit was slowly recovering. And we had a dog.

There was the awkward offer and more awkward acceptance of money from various relatives who just wanted to help.

Spring brought some work. I was writing, and my husband was acting.

I had an idea for a reality TV show proposal. It could be called "Konigland."

Five people (two parents and three children) are placed inside a small suburban house with an unrenovated kitchen, a fridge full of cold cuts, and a few suburban Blockbuster Veggie-Tales movies. There is a sprinkler in the backyard for splashing fun. Video cameras document their every move. It would be kind of a suburban *Survivor*. Sort of like MTV's *The Real World,* but with a ploppy belly.

We may not eat rats, go bungee jumping, or marry Darva Conger, but we are reality based. In fact we're more than reality based, we *are* reality. We'll give the folks at home a chance to say, "Boy, this is exactly like real life. It's uncanny."

On "Konigland" you'll:

- See me nudging a completely unwakeable husband in repeated unsuccessful attempts to convince him to get up with the baby in the middle of the night.
- See my unwakeable husband either sleeping or, even more dramatically, pretending to be asleep.
- See me trying to get ten extra minutes of sleep while various small children plead for breakfast.
- See me attempt to go to the gym—but never quite make it! (Pretty exciting stuff; we might save this one for "sweeps" week.)
- See copious quantities of Ben & Jerry's ice cream being consumed.
- See my husband worry about the greenness of his lawn.
- See him throw too much turf builder on the lawn.
- Watch as our lawn turns brown.

- See my husband being told by neighbors that he overfertilized the lawn. You'll hear little children say, "You're the best mommy in the whole, wide world." Followed by, "Can I watch TV?" followed by, "Why not?" followed by, "You're a mean mommy!" Twenty times a day.

"Konigland" is interactive! YOU, the viewer, get to choose:

- Which kid I yell at first for whining.
- What kind of chicken I make for dinner.
- Which flavor of Ben & Jerry's my husband and I will consume while sitting on the couch watching reality-based TV. (Come to think of it, you also get to choose which reality-based TV show we watch!)

"Konigland" is more than simply entertainment; it's a philosophical comment on the cultural zeitgeist, a proactive exploration of the shifting paradigms of our postmodern society. Viewers will walk away from the show forced to tackle some pretty tough questions, such as:

- Will all that laundry ever get put away or will they just keep taking things out of the dryer as needed?
- Will those breakfast dishes be washed before the week is over?
- Will that old pot of rice at the back of the fridge be

discovered and tossed before it mutates into a toxic waste hazard?

All this, and more (well, not much more) on "Konigland," the reality-based TV show so real you'll say, "Hey, that's just like reality—only it's televised!"

Maybe we could pitch it to the networks. In the meantime the bills slowly got paid. We were still sitting on top of a nice investment, dust bunnies, old kitchen, skunks, and all.

The kids were in the yard, the tulips we planted were coming up, the cat languished on the windowsill. Lulu came to visit with her new boyfriend—a Republican!—he seemed very nice.

My husband and I welcomed the first few warm nights of spring rocking on the porch with our sweet, crazy dog, who turned out to be a lab mix, not a newfie after all, and was topping out at forty-eight pounds.

Money would come. Things would work out. Life was good.

epilogue

---

the cargo space shift

One summer afternoon, when we had a quiet moment, my old pal Beth took me out to the garage and showed it to me. I'd heard about it but had never seen it—knew I'd probably never own one. She pulled back the tarp and there it was—black, of course. I was thrilled she wanted to lend it to me for our vacation.

"You just bolt it to the top of the minivan, and you can take tons more stuff."

"Just what I need to get my brood to the beach for a week." I giggled.

"Well, a van just doesn't have a lot of storage space."

I knew she was right. How had I made such an unsatisfactory automotive choice?

"But our station wagon doesn't either," she quickly added, placing a hand on my shoulder. "Especially if we're using all the seats. I guess that's why SUVs are so popular."

I perked up. "C'mon," I said, "let's put some more bug spray on the kids."

In a former life, Beth and I had lived together as swinging single chicks both in Washington, D.C., and New York City. We'd partied in a chalet in Vail, at a ranch in Palm Springs, and in a motel on Jupiter Beach.

We once went on a diet that consisted almost exclusively of beets. We gambled at the dog track. We saw a guy named Howard swim in Jell-O at a downtown performance art show. I mean, what didn't we do? From college roommates to young career girls on the go, our relationship was based on all the fun stuff we did together.

Twenty years later it's about our kids and husbands and cargo space.

After the excitement of the rooftop storage unit, we shuffled in our flip-flops back to the kiddie pool in the driveway where the children (six between us—all under eight) had been quietly slurping ice pops on a break from splashing activity.

I was still thinking about our vacation. "I'll want to pack some groceries. The supermarket at the beach is sure to be a mob scene with everything marked up for summer tourists."

"Oh, I know. Hey, remind me, I have coupons for ketchup and swim diapers."

"Great!"

Someone please help these women.

We wear sensible khaki shorts and our husbands' Polo shirts, and our idea of a wild time these days is sneaking out for an hour to indulge in a pedicure at the local strip mall. Eggplant-colored toenails, how daring!

Wasn't it just the other day that we were blasting Talking Heads, cramming shoulder pads into our blouses, and sharing copious handfuls of hair gel for wild evenings of nightclubbing?

We went out all the time whether or not we could afford it. Or we'd stay home to celebrate essential holidays like Chinese New Year by having fifty people over to our groovy, tiny, overpriced studio apartment for egg rolls. Once we'd driven fourteen hours through the night to see a basketball game in Kentucky. We invited so many people to share our hotel room that Beth ended up sleeping on the floor with a towel as a blanket. Me, I was smart and caught strep throat, developed a raging fever, and had a whole bed to myself.

But how hip were we with our big silhouettes and noisy neighbor status and our pushing-the-limits-of-logic road trips?

Now we're sitting in lawn chairs in the driveway monitoring the plastic pool and talking about the best way to remove red popsicle streaks from a toddler's belly.

Well, it didn't happen overnight. I guess I should have suspected something when Beth and her husband Carlos did the Funky Chicken at their wedding reception a few years back, and we all thought it was a riot.

But it *was* kind of cool because they just got up and weren't embarrassed and it was such a great happy day and now they have three kids and an awesome house. It's nice that things have turned out so well.

And by this point, Beth and I have survived the broken hearts, the bad jobs, the terrible apartments, the wondering if we'd ever find the right guy, settle down, have a family, a life.

As the suburban moms we are today, would we ever eat nothing but beets for a week? Not exactly a good combination of the major food groups. Pay to see a guy take a gelatin bath? Been there, done that. Drive fourteen hours to a basketball game in Kentucky? I don't think so. Although with that cargo unit bolted to the top of the minivan, it could be pretty cool.